The MLA Style Manual

Walter S. Achtert
Joseph Gibaldi

The Modern Language Association of America
New York   1985

Library of Congress Cataloging in Publication Data

Achtert, Walter S.
  The MLA style manual.
  Includes index.
  1. Authorship—Style manuals. I. Gibaldi, Joseph, 1942- . II. Modern Language Association of America. III. Title.
PN147.A28   1985   808'.02   85-4972
ISBN 0-87352-136-6

First edition
First printing, 1985, 5,500 copies
Second printing, 1986, 6,000 copies

Published by The Modern Language Association of America
10 Astor Place, New York, New York 10003

The MLA Style Manual

CONTENTS

PREFACE

For nearly half a century, journals and university presses as well as graduate schools, college departments, and individual instructors have adopted the style that the Modern Language Association of America recommends for preparing scholarly manuscripts. *The MLA Style Sheet* (1951, rev. 1970) was compiled for literary and linguistic scholars who publish in learned journals. In 1977 the *MLA Handbook for Writers of Research Papers* was published to meet the pedagogical need for a book that would incorporate the MLA style guidelines and serve as a supplementary text in writing courses or as a reference book for students to use independently. Like the *Style Sheet*, the *Handbook* was immediately adopted throughout the United States, Canada, and other countries (both works have been translated into Japanese). Indeed, the success of the *Handbook*, an amplification of the *Style Sheet*, was such that it replaced the earlier work, which soon went out of print. Thus this success ironically created the need for a new publication, a companion volume to the *Handbook*, to address the problems scholars encounter in their writing.

The recent changes in MLA style, after years of study and deliberation by various MLA committees as well as by the association's Executive Council, not only compelled a second edition of the *Handbook* (1984) but also occasioned this new manual for the scholar and graduate student, allowing us to focus the revised *Handbook* more sharply on its primary audience, the undergraduate student. *The MLA Style Manual* attempts to meet the scholar's need for a comprehensive guide to publishing in the humanities, a need enhanced during the past decade by numerous innovations affecting scholarly publication — the widespread use of word processors, a new copyright law, the adoption of anonymous-submission policies by many journals, changes in publishing techniques, and even the new MLA documentation system.

Chapter 1 addresses the broad subject of writing and publishing humanistic scholarship, covering such topics as a scholar's audiences, the genres of scholarship, appropriate language and style, plagiarism, the types of scholarly manuscripts, the stages in submitting and publishing manuscripts, relations between authors and publishers, authors' contracts, and copyright law. Chapter 2 concerns the mechanics of writing (spelling, punctuation, names of persons, capitalization, titles in manuscripts, quotations, numbers, transliteration and romanization), and chapter 3 deals with the formal preparation of the manuscript.

Chapters 4 ("Preparing the List of Works Cited") and 5 ("Documenting Sources") contain detailed instructions on using the revised MLA
documentation style. The most important change is the use of brief parenthetical citations in the text to refer to a bibliography at the end of the
article or book, thus eliminating the need for all but explanatory footnotes and endnotes. The other mechanical changes are also intended to
make scholarly documentation simpler, more consistent, and more
efficient. (For the convenience of those who write for journals and publishers that use different systems, this manual provides guidance on alternative methods, including documentation notes.) Chapter 6 treats
abbreviations, reference words, and proofreading. Chapter 7 offers advice on preparing theses and dissertations. A subject index completes the
book.

Although it would be impossible to acknowledge everyone who assisted
us with this project, we express our gratitude to a number of persons who
read and commented on drafts of the *Handbook* and the *Manual* and who
offered us valuable advice and practical suggestions: John Algeo, Richard
Bjornson, Eric J. Carpenter, Thomas Clayton, Robert A. Colby,
Richard H. Cracroft, Robert J. Di Pietro, Richard J. Dunn, Bertie E.
Fearing, John H. Fisher, John C. Gerber, Barbara Q. Gray, Martin Green,
Stephen Greenblatt, Laurel T. Hatvary, Carolyn G. Heilbrun, Weldon A.
Kefauver, Gwin J. Kolb, Richard A. LaFleur, Sarah N. Lawall, William T.
Lenehan, Richard Lloyd-Jones, William D. Lutz, Sylvia Kasey Marks,
Margaret McKenzie, Harrison T. Meserole, George J. Metcalf, Susan P.
Miller, James V. Mirollo, William G. Moulton, Judith S. Neaman, John
Neubauer, Stephen M. North, Mary Ann O'Donnell, Margaret C.
Patterson, Nancy S. Rabinowitz, James L. Rolleston, Barbara Rotundo,
Jeffrey L. Sammons, J. Thomas Shaw, Carole G. Silver, David Staines,
William R. Streitberger, Madeleine B. Therrien, Vincent L. Tollers,
Mario J. Valdés, Renée Waldinger, Jerry W. Ward, Ray Werking, Jr.,
Katharina M. Wilson, Linda L. Wyman, and Robert F. Yeager.

We would also like to give special thanks to Judith H. Altreuter, R. Neil
Beshers, Claire Cook, Judy Goulding, Elizabeth Holland, Bonnie Levy,
David Paonessa, Alex Popovkin, Hans Rütimann, Roslyn Schloss, English
Showalter, Elaine S. Silver, David Cloyce Smith, Susan Wallace, and all
our other colleagues on the MLA staff for their unfailing support and help.

1 WRITING AND PUBLICATION

1.1. Audience, genre, and the conventions of scholarship

Scholarly writing takes various shapes and forms — book reviews, journal articles, monographs, research reports — depending on the genre as well as on the audience. An accurate assessment of your intended audience will help answer many of the formal and stylistic questions that arise in preparing a manuscript. For a general audience, such as that for a book review in a newspaper, you would usually keep documentation to a minimum and give quotations only in English (regardless of the original language); for somewhat more knowledgeable readers, such as those for an article in the *American Scholar*, you might mention sources, either in the text or in a bibliography, and offer occasional words and phrases in another language, along with English translations; but a scholarly audience expects full and precise documentation and quotations in the original language (with translations subordinated, if provided at all). (See 1.2 for a discussion of the relation between audience and diction.)

This manual assumes a scholarly audience and presents suggestions and guidelines for scholarly publication. At times you may need or choose to consider variations of these suggestions; but experienced scholars, knowing that conventions by definition embody meaning readily understood by others, do not depart from them without weighing advantages against disadvantages.

In some situations, modifications result in greater clarity or enable you to meet the needs of a particular audience. Normally, you should alter established practices only by expanding them (e.g., by giving publishers' names in full or by not using abbreviations). Where conventions do not exist or are not firmly established, you should adopt clear, workable, and consistent procedures. In general, closely follow the conventions outlined in this manual when you write articles for periodicals (or essays for collections) addressed to other scholars. Longer, individual works, such as monographs, allow more latitude; other types of manuscripts, such as translations and scholarly editions, often require special practices.

1.2.   Language and style

Whereas conventions govern such matters as documentation and punctuation in scholarly manuscripts, there are no special directives for prose style. Scholars should follow the recommendations that apply to all expository prose. (The books listed in 1.3 provide guidance.) Like other authors, they should work toward writing that is direct and clear, organized and coherent, forceful and convincing. In presenting arguments, they should strive for fairness and balance while maintaining clarity and focus. In addition, they should select diction that will communicate their theses, avoiding jargon, which presumes a closed audience, and seeking instead, no matter how complex the subject, terminology comprehensible to the widest range of educated readers.

Careful writers similarly do not use language that is prejudicial to any class or category of people, avoiding statements that reflect or imply unsubstantiated generalizations about age, economic class, national origin, sexual orientation, political or religious beliefs, race, or sex. Indeed, many publishers and journals have strong editorial policies concerning the avoidance of such language. Since 1981, for example, *PMLA*'s statement of editorial policy has urged "its contributors to be sensitive to the social implications of language and to seek wording free of discriminatory overtones." In 1985, the style sheet of the Linguistic Society of America incorporated the same clause.

Discussions and statements concerning nondiscriminatory language have focused particular attention on avoiding language that could be labeled "sexist." For example, most scholarly writers no longer use "he" to refer to someone of unspecified sex. To avoid the "generic" use of "he," they recast sentences into the plural, specify the sex of an individual under discussion, and occasionally, when all else fails, use "he or she" (or "her or him"). Careful writers also avoid using English common nouns with suffixes like "-man" and "-ess" and substitute nonsexist terms (e.g., police officer, flight attendant, poet, author).

1.3.   Guides to writing

The books listed below offer writers various sorts of aid. The dictionaries of usage focus on questionable word choices and provide reasoned arguments to support their preferences. The guides to nonsexist language provide some suggestions. The books on style take up larger questions of effective communication.

Dictionaries of usage

Bernstein, Theodore. *The Careful Writer: A Modern Guide to English Usage.* New York: Atheneum, 1965.

Bryant, Margaret M. *Current American Usage: How Americans Say It and Write It.* New York: Funk, 1962.

Copperud, Roy H. *American Usage and Style: The Consensus.* New York: Van Nostrand, 1980.

Evans, Bergen, and Cornelia Evans. *Dictionary of Contemporary American Usage.* New York: Random, 1957.

Follett, Wilson. *Modern American Usage: A Guide.* Ed. Jacques Barzun. New York: Hill, 1966.

Fowler, Henry W. *A Dictionary of Modern English Usage.* Ed. Ernest Gowers. 2nd ed. New York: Oxford UP, 1965.

Nicholson, Margaret. *A Dictionary of American-English Usage Based on Fowler's Modern English Usage.* New York: Oxford UP, 1957.

Guides to nonsexist language

Cofer, Charles N., Robert S. Daniels, Frances Y. Dunham, and Walter Heimer. "Guidelines for Nonsexist Language in APA Journals." *American Psychologist* 32 (1977): 486–94.

Miller, Casey, and Kate Swift. *The Handbook of Nonsexist Writing.* New York: Lippincott, 1980.

Books on style

Beardsley, Monroe C. *Thinking Straight: Principles of Reasoning for Readers and Writers.* 4th ed. Englewood Cliffs: Prentice, 1975.

Cowan, Gregory, and Elizabeth McPherson. *Plain English Please.* 4th ed. New York: Random, 1976.

Eastman, Richard M. *Style: Writing as the Discovery of Outlook.* 2nd ed. New York: Oxford UP, 1978.

Elbow, Peter. *Writing with Power: Techniques for Mastering the Writing Process.* New York: Oxford UP, 1981.

———. *Writing without Teachers.* New York: Oxford UP, 1975.

Gibson, Walker. *Tough, Sweet, and Stuffy: An Essay on Modern American Prose Styles.* Bloomington: Indiana UP, 1966.

Gowers, Ernest. *The Complete Plain Words.* Ed. Bruce Fraser. 2nd ed. Baltimore: Penguin, 1975.

Lanham, Richard A. *Style: An Anti-Textbook.* New Haven: Yale UP, 1974.
Strunk, William, Jr., and E. B. White. *The Elements of Style.* 3rd ed. New York: Macmillan, 1979.
White, Edward M. *The Writer's Control of Tone.* New York: Norton, 1970.
Williams, Joseph M. *Style: Ten Lessons in Clarity and Grace.* Glenview: Scott, 1981.

In a category by itself, the following work guides the writer through the professional steps a copy editor takes in revising manuscripts:

Cook, Claire Kehrwald. *Line by Line: How to Edit Your Own Writing.* Boston: Houghton, 1985.

1.4. Plagiarism

Plagiarism is the use of another person's ideas or expressions in your writing without acknowledging the source. The word comes from the Latin word *plagiarius* ("kidnapper"), and Alexander Lindey defines it as "the false assumption of authorship: the wrongful act of taking the product of another person's mind, and presenting it as one's own" (*Plagiarism and Originality*, New York: Harper, 1952, 2). In short, to plagiarize is to give the impression that you have written or thought something that you have in fact borrowed from someone else, and to do so is considered a violation of the professional responsibility to acknowledge "academic debts" ("Statement on Professional Ethics," *Policy Documents and Reports*, 1984 ed., Washington: AAUP, 1984, 134).

The most blatant form of plagiarism is reproducing someone else's sentences, more or less verbatim, and presenting them as your own. Other forms include repeating another's particularly apt phrase without appropriate acknowledgment, paraphrasing someone else's argument as your own, introducing another's line of thinking as your own development of an idea, and failing to cite the source for a borrowed thesis or approach.

Plagiarism is a moral offense, rather than a legal one. Most instances of plagiarism fall outside the scope of copyright infringement (a legal offense). Simply put, plagiarism is using another person's words or ideas without appropriate acknowledgment; it makes no difference whether the work plagiarized is covered by copyright or whether the amount of material used and the nature of the use fall within the scope of fair use under the copyright law. Copyright infringement, in contrast, is using the words of a copyrighted work (or sometimes the arrangement or development of ideas) beyond the limits of fair use without the permission of the owner of the copyright. Most instances of plagiarism are not violations of the copyright law, and most violations of copyright law are not plagiarism. The penalties for plagiarism can be severe, ranging from loss of respect to loss of degrees, tenure, or even employment. At all stages of research and writing, you must guard against the possibility of inadvertent plagiarism by keeping careful notes that distinguish between your own musings and thoughts and the material you gather from others.

Even without considering the penalties of plagiarism, the best scholars generously acknowledge their debts to others. By doing so they not only contribute to the historiography of scholarship but also help younger scholars understand the process of research and discovery.

1.5. Types of scholarly manuscripts

1.5.1. Articles

Scholarly articles are of several sorts, among them factual/critical articles, book reviews, review essays, reviews of research, and research reports. Scholars also write articles for audiences not restricted to specialists in their own field; such articles may discuss, for example, the current state of understanding in a discipline or matters of public interest from the point of view of a particular discipline. The comments below on various types of scholarly articles provide broad suggestions and should, of course, be supplemented by the stated editorial policy of the journal for which you are writing.

a. Factual/critical articles

Current usage blurs the sharp distinction that was once observed between "scholarly," or factually based, articles and "critical," or theoretically based, articles. Either type requires the scholar to demonstrate familiarity with the previous scholarship on the topic, suggest an original thesis, present supporting evidence, and point to the significance of the proposition advanced. The best scholarly articles incorporate all four aspects in a proportion appropriate to the subject and audience. Failure to cover each adequately is probably the most frequent reason that journals reject articles for publication.

To demonstrate familiarity with the previous scholarship on a topic, the scholar must, of course, be certain to acquire that familiarity. Identifying the relevant scholarship is usually easier for factual articles than for theoretical articles. After locating the pertinent materials, the scholar assimilates them and relates them to the new thesis. The clearer the connections between the two, the more cogent the article. Long paragraphs—or even pages—that do little more than list the previous scholarship usually reveal that the author has not adequately assimilated it.

The thesis proposed in a scholarly article should be significant—not a refutation of another scholar's minor thesis or a trivial application of a tired theory to a work of literature. The statement of the thesis should have a prominent place in the article, and the wording should be as lucid and as concise as possible. Theses that resist clear and concise statements often have flaws and need rethinking.

After stating the thesis, the scholar should present the supporting evidence. It is often wise to begin by reviewing the categories of evidence for each aspect of the thesis, thus giving readers a sense of what will follow, and then to take up each category of evidence seriatim, making certain that the evidence is both valid and relevant to the thesis. Once all the evidence has been presented, it usually helps—except in very brief articles—to summarize the ways that the evidence supports the thesis.

Scholars often neglect the final part of the scholarly article—the significance of the thesis; yet it is this feature that ultimately commends the article to readers. The author should devote as much effort to considering and expressing the significance of the thesis as to supporting it, even though this concluding section may occupy only the final paragraph or two of the article.

b.   Book reviews

Journal editors normally commission book reviews, setting the length, arrangement, and coverage expected. Usually the work under review is fully documented at the beginning or the end of the review, but not in the usual form for a reference cited in a scholarly article. Whereas the latter need only identify a book used by the scholar, the book-review reference should inform the reader about the availability of a recently published book. It is common to record all the information included on the title page; to give the pagination, price, and binding (cloth, paper); to indicate how to order the book if it is not published by a major press; and to include information about publication in other countries (often noted on the verso of the title page of the work).

At its best, a book review is both informative and evaluative, describing the book's contents and assessing its significance, accuracy, and cogency. Reviewers given little space must take particular care to present a balanced examination of the work.

c.   Review essays

Review essays are extended book reviews, usually covering more than one book and giving full publication information for each work discussed. Like book reviews, they are generally commissioned. Review articles normally allow the writer greater compass to describe and compare the works under consideration and to place them in perspective. On occasion, reviewers use such assignments as the impetus for original factual/critical articles, sometimes to the neglect of the information readers expect to find in a review.

d.   Reviews of research

Like book reviews and review articles, the review of research is usually commissioned by a journal editor or a book editor. Unlike the other two, however, the review of research generally provides only the normal scholarly documentation of its sources. The reviewer, often allotted inadequate space for the task, attempts to recognize the significant works in a field, to indicate their contents, and to evaluate them, justifying the evaluations wherever possible. Models of judiciousness and tight prose, the best reviews of research contribute enormously to the development of their scholarly fields, often setting the terms of discussion for future work.

e.   Research reports

University research programs and government agencies now fund much research in the humanities; sometimes government agencies or private foundations ask scholars to investigate matters of public interest. To meet the conditions of such funding, researchers often have to file reports on the work they have done. The research report must usually follow a prescribed outline and must often describe the precise means by which the research was carried out (questionnaires were sent to n departments, responses were received from *n* departments, and so forth). Scholars should not let the mechanical requirements of a research report and the need to describe their procedures dominate their thinking to such an extent that they focus their writing more on the apparatus of research than on its meaning. Research reports, like all writing, should attempt to communicate significant information to educated readers.

1.5.2. Books

This manual discusses, in addition to monographs, three of the many types of books scholars produce: collections of original essays, collections of reprinted essays, and reference works, each of which has some special features not common to all scholarly writing. The details of preparing a scholarly edition are beyond the scope of this manual. For precise guidance, consult the vast literature in the field. For a brief guide to that literature, see *The Center for Scholarly Editions: An Introductory Statement* (New York: MLA, 1977); for a basic introduction to the field, see William Proctor Williams and Craig S. Abbott, *An Introduction to Bibliographical and Textual Studies* (New York: MLA, 1985).

In preparing any type of book, give careful consideration to the likely publisher of the manuscript, for book publishers are far fewer than journal publishers and the effort involved in revising or recasting a manuscript to meet a publisher's requirements can often be herculean. Early planning and careful attention to the suggestions of potential publishers can significantly ease the transition from manuscript to published book. (See 1.6–7 for a description of the steps from submission to publication.)

a. Monographs

The most common form of scholarly book, the monograph is an extended discussion of a restricted topic, generally by a single author but occasionally by a small team in close collaboration. The author usually begins with a clear statement of thesis, expressed in a paragraph or two, and then explores that thesis by analyzing a significant body of evidence. In many branches of the humanities, the monograph is the primary means of advancing scholarly knowledge. A number of publishers have established monograph series, grouping titles according to subject matter.

b. Collections of original essays

At its best, a collection of original essays by different authors offers readers a breadth of knowledge and a diversity of perspective and methodology that no book by a single author can offer. But precisely because of the numerous minds and personalities involved, edited books of essays are particularly vulnerable to disunity, incoherence, unevenness, and confusion of purpose. This section discusses collections with unified contents; collections with eclectic contents, such as proceedings of conferences and compilations of essays to honor scholars or public occasions, resemble issues of journals.

The editor of a collection conceived as a unified book bears ultimate responsibility for its success or failure. Far from being a mere collector and introducer of essays, the editor of a collaborative volume must define and shape the book from its conception to its publication. Specifically, the editor must identify a useful and important subject for the book, establish clear and attainable objectives, define the intended audience, divide the book's subject into topics, select appropriate contributors, assign specific topics, establish unambiguous guidelines for writing the essays, maintain high scholarly and editorial standards, and, perhaps most important of all, communicate these goals and expectations to contributors.

Long before approaching a publisher or inviting contributors, the prospective editor of a book of original essays should consult widely with colleagues to help ascertain whether, in fact, there is a scholarly or professional market for the projected book and, if there is, exactly what kind of book is needed, what topics should be included, and which contributors might be invited. After preparing a prospectus or outline to send to a potential publisher, the editor may approach some of the possible contributors for tentative commitments. Including the names of possible contributors in the prospectus will help the publisher and its consultants evaluate the proposal. But the editor should not formally invite anyone to contribute until a publisher expresses serious interest in the projected book and invites a manuscript.

Having attracted a publisher, the editor sends formal invitations to the chosen contributors. Since one or more of the potential authors may not accept, the editor should have qualified alternative contributors in mind for all topics. The invitations should spell out clearly and explicitly the precise assignment for each contributor and include a set of general guidelines for writing the essays. The guidelines should cover the overall objectives of the book, the intended audience, the organization and length of the essay (if essays are to be uniform), the documentation style, the deadlines, editorial procedures, and the editor's right to reject, or to ask the author to revise, any manuscript that does not meet requirements or that falls short of the quality expected.

While awaiting submission of essays, the editor may begin drafting an introduction to the book, but such a piece usually has to be modified, after all the essays have been collected, to reflect the actual contents of the volume. This time may also be profitably spent in preparing a preliminary bibliography for the work.

After receiving contributors' essays, the editor must check to see that each fulfills the assignment and conforms to the guidelines. Concerned with substance as well as with style, the editor should not only review the essays for unity, coherence, clarity, and cogency but seek the advice and expertise of colleagues in the field, asking appropriate scholars to read and comment on parts or all of the manuscript. In addition, the conscientious editor will verify all references and bibliographic citations. This preliminary editing, which usually takes several months, should go on with the full knowledge, cooperation, and participation of contributors. When finally satisfied with the individual contributions and with the work as a whole, the editor submits the manuscript to the publisher for evaluation.

On the basis of readers' reports and evaluation by the acquiring editor and the appropriate editorial committee or board, the publisher will usually either approve the manuscript for publication or ask for substantial revision. If the manuscript is returned for revision, the editor needs once again to work with individual contributors to put the manuscript in publishable form. Even if the manuscript is approved, the publisher will probably ask for some final revision before copyediting. In either instance, readers' reports and the publisher's advice are the best guides to follow.

When submitting the manuscript for copyediting, the editor should provide the mailing addresses and telephone numbers of all contributors, so that the publisher can send each contributor a contract, the relevant portions of the copyedited manuscript and galley proofs, and any compensation, such as an honorarium, complimentary copies of the book, or a royalty. The editor normally receives a complete set of galley proofs for the volume and, especially if an index is required, a complete set of page proofs. (Some publishers send the editor the complete copyedited manuscript instead of distributing the appropriate portions to individual contributors.) See 1.7.4 for guidance on handling proofs and 1.7.5 for advice on preparing an index.

It is essential for the editor of a book of original essays to maintain clear, readily accessible lines of communication with contributors. The editor should regularly send letters, memos, and progress reports to all contributors at every stage during the preparation of the book: to remind contributors of imminent (or past) deadlines, acknowledge receipt of material, request revision or offer editorial suggestions, explain delays or other changes in schedule, congratulate and praise work well done, and announce significant news concerning the submission, evaluation, and publication of the manuscript. Continual communication helps to avoid confusion and misunderstanding and enhances the possibility of successful collaboration.

c. Collections of previously published essays

Collections of previously published essays, bringing together significant studies from diverse sources, are convenient volumes for individual researchers and libraries that may not own the journals and books from which the essays are drawn. A scholar interested in preparing such a work as part of a series, with its own focus and requirements, should examine the earlier collections to see whether they overlap and to ascertain the publisher's expectations.

The manuscript of a collection of previously printed essays, as submitted to the publisher, normally consists of photocopies of the printed essays marked for typographical corrections (often made "silently" in the reprinting) and any other required changes, a list of acknowledgments for the rights to reprint the essays, a table of contents, an introduction, and often a bibliography. Although the holders of the rights to the essays may specify no more than a general acknowledgment, editors of such collections should provide, as a service to other scholars, full bibliographic information about the original publications.

d. Reference works

Reference works are normally prepared only under contract to a publisher, since they usually involve an enormous investment of time and close cooperation between author and publisher. Unlike monographs or collections of original essays, reference works must adhere to relatively strict editorial policies and must follow numerous conventions that will make them readily accessible to their users. Scholars should not undertake such large-scale projects without first consulting with potential publishers.

1.6.   Submitting the manuscript

1.6.1.   Selecting the appropriate publisher

One of the keys to successful scholarly publication is locating the appropriate publisher. Whether you are seeking a journal for an article or a book publisher for a monograph, nothing can be so discouraging as receiving rejection after rejection—an experience you can avoid by not approaching inappropriate publishers. The traditional advice about finding a suitable publisher is to read through annual bibliographies to note who has published articles or books in your field. While that advice is useful, it sometimes sends scholars to publishers who are now looking for material in quite different areas.

Fortunately, if you are seeking an appropriate journal for an article, you can consult directories to the editorial policies of journals in many fields. The *MLA Directory of Periodicals*, for example, provides brief summaries of the editorial policies of journals and series in languages and literatures. Once you have selected potential journals for your article, you should consult their current issues to learn about recent changes in editorial policy, special interests, and the details of submission procedures. Although the *MLA Directory of Periodicals* provides information on submission procedures, the short time it takes to check recent issues of the journals will be well spent if it forestalls even one rejection on technical grounds.

Locating appropriate book publishers is more difficult, since the directories of book publishers (such as the annual *Literary Market Place*) do not provide detailed information on the publishers' editorial policies. You have to consult colleagues and the annual bibliographies to learn which publishers are currently interested in the topic and the method you have chosen.

1.6.2.   The prospectus or outline

Few publishers have the time or staff to read unsolicited manuscripts, and it is usually better to send a brief letter and a prospectus or outline than to submit a complete manuscript uninvited. (Since journals regularly print their editorial guidelines and submission requirements, editors expect authors to follow those procedures and not to send letters of inquiry or outlines not specified in the policy statements.)

The prospectus or outline for a book-length manuscript should clearly and succinctly state the goals and purposes of the manuscript and include descriptions, each about a paragraph long, of the need for the book, the audience, the qualities that distinguish the book, and the thesis and how it will be developed. The prospectus should also indicate how much of the book is finished and when, realistically, completion can be expected. In addition, it should include a résumé of the author's relevant experience and publications (résumés listing all an author's activities and publications usually go unread).

The cover letter accompanying the prospectus or outline should be an original, not a duplicate. It should indicate whether the prospectus is currently being considered by another publisher and, without exaggerating the merits of the proposed book, should attempt to interest its recipient in publishing the book. Bear in mind that this letter, along with the prospectus or outline, will most likely be sent to consultant readers and editorial committees.

On receiving a prospectus or outline, an editor will usually read it quickly to ascertain whether the proposed book falls within the scope of the publishing program. (Letters that are duplicated, with or without the name of the publisher typed in, and those that show no awareness of the publisher's programs are often neither read nor acknowledged.) If the proposed book falls outside the publishing program or if the proposal seems ill-conceived, the editor will normally reject it immediately with a brief note stating that the book does not meet the publisher's current requirements. Otherwise, the editor will read the proposal more carefully, perhaps circulate it to consultants, and eventually present it to whoever has the authority to make even tentative commitments. Depending on the publisher and the time of year, this process may take anywhere from one month to six; if the proposal indicates that the work is complete, the editor, without consulting widely, may invite the author to submit the manuscript for full consideration.

At some point, an editor will either report to the author that the book proposal is no longer being considered or ask to see the complete manuscript, sometimes offering a contract for publication at this point (see 1.7.1 concerning contracts). Often such a request will be accompanied by suggestions for changes in the proposed book; an author should evaluate those suggestions carefully before agreeing to follow them. Although publishers' editors and their consultants have a wealth of experience in both scholarship and publishing that authors should not disregard lightly, editors and consultants do make mistakes, and authors sometimes acquiesce to erroneous suggestions when they ought to seek a publisher more sympathetic to their own ideas.

1.6.3.   Preparation of the manuscript

Prepare manuscripts according to the technical specifications given in chapter 3 of this manual or specified by the publisher. Be especially careful that all pages are numbered and in order (see 3.1), that your name does not appear inappropriately in manuscripts to be considered under anonymous-submissions policies (see 3.2.1), and that you have the requisite membership status for a journal published by an association.

Beyond attending to these technical requirements, make certain that the manuscript you are about to submit is indeed a manuscript you wish to have published in its present form. Is it accurate and "finished"? Recheck all quotations and bibliographic references; and if you discover that an edition cited is not the most recent or most authoritative, adopt the more appropriate one, make all necessary changes in direct quotations, and determine whether any differences between this edition and the edition originally cited require changes in the thesis or argument of the manuscript. You should also review scholarship published since you began writing the manuscript and make appropriate modifications. In short, though you will have later opportunities for revision, you should make the manuscript you submit as close as possible to the one you would like to see published.

1.6.4.   Submission of the manuscript

For a book manuscript, follow the publisher's instructions, if any, on the method of shipment and the number of copies to be submitted. Always keep a copy of the manuscript for yourself.

For a manuscript of an article, follow the instructions printed in the journal concerning the number of copies to be submitted, submission fees, the need for return postage, and any information the author is expected to provide along with the manuscript. Always keep a copy of the manuscript for yourself.

An editor will usually acknowledge receipt of a manuscript within a reasonable time, depending on the season and the publisher.

1.6.5.   Readers' reports and revisions

To evaluate the appropriateness of a manuscript for publication, most editors will send a manuscript to a number of consultant readers, sometimes simultaneously and sometimes consecutively. Although the specific questions asked of consultant readers vary from journal to journal and publisher to publisher, most editors request (1) a brief statement of the scope and purpose of the manuscript, (2) an assessment of the accuracy and originality of the scholarship, (3) an assessment of the importance of the work and, for a book manuscript, a statement about the potential audience, (4) for a book manuscript, a comparison of the manuscript with other books on the subject, (5) comments on the style and organization of the manuscript, often including recommendations for cutting, and (6) suggestions for improvement. Although many publishers ask consultants whether they favor publication of the manuscript, others ask only for specific information. Some publishers also ask consultants to suggest other journals or houses that might be more appropriate for the manuscript.

Consultant readers for journals in the humanities usually receive no compensation for their services, though some journals list them periodically or appoint them as consulting editors. Consultant readers of book-length manuscripts are usually paid honoraria depending on the length and complexity of the manuscripts they evaluate. When asked to prepare a report for a publisher, a consultant should conscientiously try to cover the points the editor has raised, recognizing that the report will be read carefully by an editorial committee deciding for or against publication and that it will also be sent to the author.

In securing such evaluations, editors receive suggestions on ways to improve the manuscript. It is a rare manuscript that is accepted for publication with no revisions. After reviewing the consultants' reports, an editor will often return the manuscript to the author with an invitation to revise and resubmit it. To avoid considerable misunderstanding and ill will, both the editor and the author should pay close attention to the wording of such invitations. Editors who do not mean to promise anything other than a reading of a revised manuscript should be certain that they do not, in their eagerness to avoid offending the author, imply automatic acceptance. Authors eager to have a manuscript accepted should not read more into an invitation than is warranted.

Even the most experienced authors have difficulty responding well to other than glowing reports from readers. Having invested considerable thought and time in their manuscripts, authors often react defensively to the readers' reports. The advice of colleagues and friends can help sort out useful suggestions from misunderstandings (and can point to the sources of the misunderstandings). Allowing several days to pass between receiving the readers' reports and beginning to compare the reports with the manuscript can often help overcome initial reluctance to accept any criticisms the readers have offered.

An author who decides to undertake the revisions requested should so inform the editor and report on the progress being made. Otherwise there may be some unhappy surprises: an editor who does not hear from an author assumes that the manuscript has been sent elsewhere and may have little interest when the revised manuscript comes in a year later. In reviewing a work that has been revised for reconsideration, most editors request copies of all the previous correspondence and sometimes a copy of the earlier version of the manuscript. When returning a revised manuscript to an editor, explain in an accompanying letter exactly which recommended changes you have made and which you have not, giving explicit reasons for your rejections.

1.7.   Publishing the manuscript

1.7.1.   Acceptance and contracts

At some point after it has been favorably evaluated by consultant readers, editors, and editorial board members, a manuscript is formally accepted for publication, either as is or subject to revisions that do not require further review by the editorial board (it is this sort of request for revision that authors sometimes mistakenly think they have received when they have in fact been requested to revise the manuscript so that it can be resubmitted to the editorial board). Even manuscripts that are accepted without need for revision are usually returned to their authors at this time for any updating or final improvements their authors wish to make. Authors should make any requested revisions and carefully observe any deadlines their editors send them, for from this point forward their manuscripts are but individual parts of a complex whole, whether they are manuscripts scheduled for an issue of a journal or for separate publication in a particular season.

After accepting a manuscript, the journal or book publisher usually offers the author a contract, or memorandum of agreement, for publication of the manuscript. Some scholarly book publishers, like most trade book publishers, offer contracts when they approve a prospectus, but although these contracts specify the terms under which the publisher will compensate the author, they do not guarantee publication, since they usually stipulate that the manuscript be satisfactory to the publisher "in form and content." Authors need to remember that a publishing contract is a legal document that, although limited by copyright law, is a binding transfer of rights and usually an obligation to undertake certain activities. Many authors make the mistake of not reading their contracts until they are unpleasantly surprised (e.g., when the publisher sends fewer author copies of the work than they had hoped to receive or when their royalties do not arrive on the first of the year).

Contracts for the publication of a scholarly article range from rather informal letters stating the journal's practices to more formal agreements stipulating terms. Without a document that can be considered a legal contract, no transfer of copyright rights takes place. United States copyright law then governs the relation between author and publisher: "In the absence of an express transfer of the copyright or of any rights under it, the owner of copyright in the collective work is presumed to have acquired only the privilege of reproducing and distributing the contribution as part of that particular collective work, any revision of that collective work, and any later collective work in the same series" (17 US Code, sec. 201(c), 1976). The usual points covered in any such contract are the author's warranty that the manuscript is original, is not the work of anyone else, has not been published previously, and infringes the rights of no one; the grant of rights to the publisher, either the full transfer of some or all of the rights collectively known as "copyright" or the specific authorization to publish the manuscript in the journal; the publisher's agreement to publish the manuscript; the author's agreement to read and return proofs to the publisher; and the compensation, most often in the form of offprints or copies of the journal, to be given to the author and the manner in which subsidiary income — for example, from permissions to reprint — will be divided if the author's grant of rights allows the publisher to permit others to reprint the material. Journal editors and authors of articles should make certain that they are in clear agreement about each of these major points, which are discussed below in the context of contracts for book-length manuscripts.

Contracts for publication of book-length manuscripts are usually more elaborate than those for articles. Typically, an author (1) grants rights to the publisher; (2) authorizes registering the copyright for the material; and (3) warrants that he or she is the sole owner of the material and indemnifies the publisher against suits and claims. The author also agrees (4) to deliver the manuscript; (5) to read and return proofs; (6) to pay the costs of alterations above a stated amount; (7) to undertake revisions for subsequent editions; (8) to offer other manuscripts to the publisher and not to offer competing manuscripts to another publisher; (9) to provide an index, illustrations, and other supplementary materials; and (10) to secure permission to use copyrighted materials. The publisher commonly agrees (11) to publish the work within a reasonable period of time, (12) to provide compensation to the author, and (13) to provide copies of the published work to the author. The author and the publisher commonly agree on (14) termination of the contract and (15) the addresses to be used for required notifications. In addition, most contracts contain clauses concerning the succession of rights and the laws under which the contract is to be interpreted. Often, for convenience in keeping records, publishers will include in the contract (16) the author's social security number, date of birth, and country of citizenship. Each of these aspects of a typical contract is discussed below.

(1) The author's grant of rights to the publisher. A typical publishing contract calls for the author to "grant and assign" to the publisher "any and all" rights associated with the work for "any and all" purposes in "any and all" languages. Although authors who wish to can usually persuade their publishers to reword the contract so that the only rights granted are those the publisher expects to exercise (e.g., serial publication, book publication, reprint, translation, and perhaps electronic adaptation), the remaining rights often have no apparent value, and authors are frequently reluctant to appear difficult before a contract is signed.

(2) Authorization to register the copyright of the work. A typical contract authorizes the publisher to register the copyright of the work either in its name or in the name of the author, usually depending on which rights have been transferred to the publisher, and guarantees that the author will execute any papers necessary. It is generally more convenient to have the copyright registered in the name of the publisher if the publisher either owns or controls the subsidiary rights.

(3) The warranty and indemnity. Typically, the author is asked to warrant that the work is original, that he or she is the sole author and has full power to make the agreement, that the work has not been published previously, and that it is not the subject of any other publishing agreement. The typical warranty clause then lists a series of adjectives that the author warrants the work is not: libelous, unlawful, invasive of the privacy of others, and so forth. The author "indemnifies and holds harmless" the publisher against, usually, any and all suits or claims (and often a series of similar nouns) that the publisher might possibly be subjected to because of the work.

(4) Agreement to deliver a satisfactory manuscript. The author typically agrees to deliver a manuscript of a specified length, in a specified number of legible copies, on or before a certain date, "time being of the essence," often together with such supplements as "illustrations, maps, and charts" (typically qualified as "reproducible without redrawing"), the quantity of such illustrations usually restricted. The agreement to deliver the manuscript generally stipulates that it will be satisfactory to the publisher in form, substance, and content. Authors should read this section of their contracts with care, noting particularly the date by which they

must provide the manuscript, the definition, if any, of a satisfactory manuscript, and any agreement to provide illustrations. The phrase "time being of the essence" enables the publisher to cancel the contract if the author does not deliver the manuscript by the date specified.

(5) Reading and returning proofs. The author typically agrees to read, correct, and return proofs within a certain number of days after the publisher has mailed them to the author and further agrees that the publisher may proceed to publish the manuscript if the author does not return the proofs within this period. The typical contract does not oblige the publisher to accept any of the author's changes in proof and provides that the publisher may charge the author for the cost of proofreading should the author fail to read and return proofs.

(6) Costs of alterations. The typical contract calls for an author to pay the costs of alterations to the galley or page proofs that exceed a stated percentage of the cost of the original typesetting. Typical percentages range from 5% to 10%, but more and more publishers are lowering these percentages and exercising this clause in an attempt to hold down costs. Some publishers, however, exercise this clause only in extreme situations; others do not allow any changes in proof except to correct errors of the compositor. Since compositors calculate the costs of author's alterations in a variety of ways (e.g., by line or by time spent) and since one change may necessitate resetting an entire paragraph, an author usually cannot estimate the number and nature of changes that will fall within the allowable percentages. Since changes in proof slow down production and frequently lead to additional errors, authors should keep corrections to a minimum (see 1.7.4).

(7) Subsequent editions. Many contracts stipulate that the author will undertake revisions requested by the publisher for subsequent editions of the work and that if the author fails to do so the publisher can arrange to have such revisions made, charging the cost to the author's royalties.

(8) Other manuscripts. A contract sometimes contains an "option" clause, which ensures the publisher an opportunity to offer a contract on any future manuscript by the author. Such option clauses are rare in scholarly book contracts and are not usually exercised even when they do appear. A contract may also contain a clause, common in contracts for textbooks, prohibiting the author from submitting to another publisher any work that would compete with the work in question.

(9) Indexes and similar material. Typically, an author is asked to agree to provide an index for the book within a stated number of days after receiving page proofs from the publisher, with the provision that if the author fails to do so the publisher will have an index prepared and charge the cost to the author's royalty account. Some contracts also mention "simi-

lar material" that the author agrees to prepare; authors would be wise to clarify with their publishers exactly what similar material they must provide and to insist on specific language in the contract.

(10) Permission to use copyrighted material. The contract generally assigns to the author the obligation and the cost of securing permission to use copyrighted material. (See 1.9.2 concerning permissions.)

(11) The publisher's agreement to publish the work. Typically the publisher agrees to publish the manuscript (following approval by an editorial board, if the contract is issued before such approval) in "such manner and style" as the publisher deems "best," at the publisher's expense (except as provided elsewhere in the contract). The publisher's agreement to publish makes the publisher the sole arbiter of an acceptable manuscript and the appropriate design and content for the book and usually gives the publisher the sole right to set the price of the work.

(12) Compensation to the author. Typically, the contract offers to compensate the author at rates varying for each source of potential income from the manuscript. The sources of income include domestic as well as export sales of a clothbound edition, domestic as well as export sales of a paperbound edition, direct-mail sales of any edition, and the licensing of subsidiary rights (e.g., reprints of the whole work or portions thereof, translations, and movie rights). Publishers vary in what they use as the royalty "base": some compute royalties on the list price, others on net income from sales, still others on a specified percentage of the list price or on an "invoice price." Since definitions of the words that describe the royalty base vary, scholars should ask publishers for clarification if the amount of royalty is an important consideration. The royalty offered on a clothbound edition is often higher than that offered on a paperbound edition. Some publishers pay the same royalty rate for all copies sold; others use a sliding scale, paying a higher royalty after certain numbers of copies have been sold. The rates offered, of course, vary considerably, depending on the publisher's estimate of the commercial potential of the work. For scholarly books, it is not uncommon for the publisher to pay no royalty at all on the first 500, 1,000, or even 1,500 copies. (Publishers often use the additional income they gain on these books to pay the original costs of composition and printing, thus enabling them to keep prices of books printed in small quantities within an affordable range.) The customary rates paid on domestic sales of clothbound editions range from 7½% to 15%. Rates for export sales range from one-half to two-thirds the amount for domestic sales, and rates for paperbound editions are often about one-half those paid for clothbound editions. Typically, a publisher will pay an author 50% of the net receipts from subsidiary rights.

For books with multiple authors, the publisher will divide the royalties or sometimes pay an honorarium in lieu of royalties.

(13) Author's copies. Most contracts oblige the publisher to provide a specified number of copies of the published work to the author at no charge and grant the author the right to purchase additional copies at a stated discount from the list price in effect at the time of the purchase. Sometimes this provision states that any such copies purchased by the author are not to be resold. Authors who need many copies (for university and foundation officials, colleagues, relatives, and friends) should read this portion of the contract with care. Although an author can often negotiate a higher number of author's copies with a publisher before signing a contract, perhaps by trading a lower royalty percentage for a higher number of copies, these factors enter into the publisher's financial plan for the work and usually cannot be changed later.

(14) Termination of the contract. Many contracts give the publisher the right to terminate the contract after a stated number of years following publication of the work, often with the provision that the author be allowed at that time to purchase any remaining stock of the work. If the author declines to purchase it, the publisher is free to dispose of it at will.

(15) The addresses to be used for required notifications. Many contracts prescribe the means of transmitting required notices from one party to the other, often providing that notices be sent by registered mail to stated addresses.

(16) The author's social security number, date of birth, and country of citizenship. Publishers frequently request that the contract show the author's social security number, date of birth, and country of citizenship. A publisher needs the social security number to file reports on royalties paid, the date of birth to record the work correctly in the Library of Congress, and the country of citizenship to register the copyright.

1.7.2.   Final revisions

After accepting a manuscript, the publishers may return it to the author for final revisions. Sometimes the publisher will make certain types of revisions a condition of accepting the manuscript; at other times, the publisher will allow the author to decide which revisions and updatings seem appropriate. When requesting revisions, the publisher will often give the author copies of the readers' reports and summarize the editorial committee's comments. Using these guides, the author should make the final revisions as rapidly as possible, so that publication of the work can proceed.

1.7.3. Copyediting

No step in the publishing process seems to raise as many problems as copyediting does. Done well, it greatly improves the quality of a scholarly work by identifying stylistic weaknesses that impair readability and by correcting errors of logic or fact that have escaped the author's attention. Done poorly, it creates annoyances and difficulties for the author and can result in inferior publications. Unfortunately, instead of striving to improve the copyediting of scholarly works, many publishers, trying to reduce costs, no longer provide extensive copyediting services, relying on authors to play amateur copy editors.

Arthur Plotnik, in *The Elements of Editing: A Modern Guide for Editors and Journalists* (New York: Macmillan, 1982), records questions that come to his mind if copy editors seem to finish their work too quickly. Although he is referring primarily to writing for popular magazines, his questions apply equally well to scholarly publications:

- Have they weighed every phrase and sentence of the script to determine whether the author's meaning will be carried to the intended audience?
- Have they measured every revision they propose to make against the advantages of the author's original voice and presentation?
- Have they pondered the effectiveness of every phrase to the limits of their grammatical ear—and then beyond, with two or three modern-usage guides at hand?
- Have they studied every possible area of numerical, factual, or judgmental error until they can swear that to the best of their knowledge and research this manuscript is accurate and ready to be immortalized in print?
- Have they strained their eyes for typos and transpositions, especially in those parts of the manuscript retyped or reorganized? Have they edited and proofread their own editing as well?
- Have they . . . groveled in the details of the footnotes, tables, and appendices until every last em-dash, en-dash, and subscript is marked, every parenthesis is closed, and all abbreviations and italicizations are consistent?
- Have they cast a legal eye upon every quoted phrase, defamatory comment, trade name, allegation, and attribution, whether it appears in footnote, caption, dedication, title page, or main text?
- Have they stepped back to consider the impact of the whole as well as the parts, tuned an ear to overtones of sexism, racism,

ageism, ethnocentrism, and any other isms that will undermine the intentions of the author and publisher or unintentionally alienate the reader?

- Have they, if required, provided all the editorial embellishments to the text — title, subtitle, subheads, author notes, editorial notes, sidebars, blowups, dingbats, and instructions to the designer?
- Have they, if it is the policy of the publication, cleared every significant revision and addition with the author? (35–36)

A copy editor's mission, then, ranges over the gamut of publishing responsibilities, from helping the author communicate effectively and providing the "embellishments" the publisher wishes for the manuscript to protecting the author (who signed the clause holding the publisher harmless in case of suit) from legal complications. Still, the complaints of authors against copy editors are legion, and the examples copy editors can offer of what their authors would have them "stet" give cause for worry about the state of contemporary culture. Yet surely not all authors are ignorant (if they were, why would their publishers publish them?), and not all copy editors are failed authors trying to impose their own voices on every manuscript they touch (if they were, why would publishers hire them?).

One cause of frequent misunderstanding is the imposition of "house style" on manuscripts: the editing of spelling, forms for numbers, capitalization, italicization, and the like. Since these matters are somewhat arbitrary, authors often feel they should arbitrate. Whatever arguments authors bring against house style, they fall before the very practical argument in its favor: it is the only way a publisher can ensure consistency both within a work and from work to work, and without such consistency readers will be left to puzzle the significance of the variations.

Most publishers return a copyedited manuscript to the author to get responses to the proposed changes and to obtain answers to questions. In reviewing the copyedited manuscript, the author should remember that the copy editor is most likely a skilled professional who has not suggested changes for whimsical reasons. The author should carefully evaluate each suggested change and either accept it or substitute a different revision (simply writing "stet" rarely resolves the problem but merely passes it over to galley proofs or later correspondence). No matter how inane, naive, or irrelevant a copy editor's question may seem, an author should attempt to answer all queries (and must not erase or otherwise obliterate any of them). Experienced copy editors usually explain questions or changes that do not seem self-explanatory, but sometimes, particularly when they are pressed for time, they will offer no explanation; experienced authors usually take it as a matter of faith that there is a reason for the change. Reproduced below is a portion of the manuscript of this manual as copyedited by Claire Cook and Roslyn Schloss.

@ptxt@~~Following completion of copyediting,~~ most publishers return a copyedited manuscript to ~~its~~ [the] author to get ~~reactions~~ [responses] to the proposed changes and to obtain answers to questions[.] ~~that have arisen.~~ ~~Responding to~~ [In reviewing] the copyedited manuscript[,] ~~requires~~ the author ~~to~~ [should] remember that the copy[#]editor is most likely a skilled ~~individual~~ [professional] who has not suggested changes for whimsical reasons. [The author should carefully evaluate] Each suggested change ~~should be evaluated carefully by the author~~ and either accepted or ~~a~~ substitute [it] ~~offered in its stead~~ [a different revision] (~~in most instances, when an author merely~~ [simply] writ~~es~~[ing] @oq@stet@cq@ [the problem ~~is not resolved,~~ [rarely resolves] [but] merely passe[s] it over to galley proof[s] or later correspondence). No matter how inane, naive, or irrelevant a [copy editor's] question may seem, an author should attempt to answer all ~~of the copyeditor's questions~~ [queries] (and must not erase or otherwise obliterate any of them). Experienced copy[#]editors usually explain ~~the reason for each~~ question[s] or change[s] [that do not seem self-explanatory,] ~~but~~ sometimes, particularly when they are pressed for time[,] ~~or the reason seems obvious,~~ they will offer no explanation; experienced authors usually take it as a matter of faith that there is a ~~compelling~~ reason ~~to make a~~ [for the] change.

Before returning the copyedited manuscript to the publisher, the author should make sure that all questions are answered and all requested information supplied—and, most important, that all needed changes are made. From this point forward, changes become costly (and are often charged to the author or not even made). It is therefore important to review the copyediting carefully, but every effort should be made to return the manuscript to the editor within the time agreed on, or as quickly as possible if no schedule has been set.

1.7.4. Proofreading

Having passed the hurdle of reviewing the copyedited manuscript, the author shortly thereafter receives a set of galley proofs, usually along with the manuscript. For most journal articles and many books, galley proofs are the last an author sees of the work before the printed product. Because changes at this stage can not only prove costly (usually to the author) but also seriously delay a publishing schedule, the author should explain the relative importance of any desired corrections, so that the publisher can make informed decisions about allowing them. Most publishers will not authorize stylistic refinements at this stage but will usually make changes to remove factual errors.

Read galley proofs word for word against the manuscript. If you are not an experienced proofreader, it may help to have someone else read the manuscript aloud while you read the proofs. Use appropriate proofreading symbols in making corrections (see 6.8), and respond clearly to any queries from the editor or typesetter.

1.7.5. Preparing an index

Preparing the index for a scholarly book is usually the author's responsibility, and the task entails both intellectual stimulation and sheer drudgery. In negotiating the contract, the author and the editor should determine the sort of index required: for example, an index of names, an index of both names and concepts, or even various kinds of indexes. The purpose, scope, and audience of the index should all receive careful consideration before preparation begins; it would be inappropriate in a work on German philology, for example, to index German words under their translations and equally inappropriate in a cookbook to index "salmon" under *Salmo salar.*

An author can start working on the index at any point in the development of the manuscript, but the most useful stage is often the four to six weeks between returning galley proofs and receiving page proofs. In that period an author can usually mark a set of galley proofs with the appropriate terms for indexing; because deadlines usually exert considerable pressure, an author could even type index cards or slips of paper at this time (of course, without the page numbers) and, most important, decide on the appropriate heads and subheads.

The procedure recommended here makes it convenient to begin preparing the index at any time and to retain copies of the work done at each stage. It is important to keep such copies, because entries discovered with erroneous or missing page references usually have to be discarded if there are no records enabling the indexer to retrace the correct numbers.

To prepare an index, work from either a copy of the manuscript or a set of galley proofs. Carefully indicate the words and phrases to be indexed and add in the margins words and phrases that do not appear in the work but that should appear in the index. Mark on the manuscript or proof any phrase that will need to be inverted in the index. Assign each word or phrase an appropriate subheading (to guard against the possibility of ending up with index headings followed by long strings of undifferentiated page numbers; you can later discard subheadings that prove needless). Then type the headings seriatim on 8½ by 11″ sheets of paper, skipping six lines between headings and numbering the sheets. When page proofs arrive, read these sheets against the page proofs, make any needed additions, and mark the appropriate page numbers next to each heading. Read through the entire set of sheets to make certain that each heading has a page number (and that the page number makes sense; that is, if it differs from the page number of the preceding or following heading, it should differ by only one page). Photocopy these sheets and save the photocopies. Cut the original sheets into small slips of paper with one heading, subheading, and page number on each slip. Alphabetize these slips. Edit them to remove unnecessary subheadings and add slips for "see" and "see also" references. Then, working from these slips (either loose or taped to large sheets of paper for convenience), type the final index copy double-spaced and in one column. Although most indexes are printed in run-in style, it is usually clearer to prepare the copy in indented style (with each subhead on a separate line indented under the major head).

The procedure described above was suggested in Kenneth L. Pike, "How to Make an Index," *PMLA* 83 (1968): 991-93. *The Chicago Manual of Style* (13th ed., Chicago: U of Chicago P, 1982) recommends typing individual index cards for each entry (a time-consuming procedure that leaves no way of tracing errors) and briefly defines various kinds of indexes. Scholars working with computers can facilitate the preparation of indexes by recording the headings, subheadings, and page numbers, using any applications program capable of sorting this material. They can also use special indexing programs if their manuscripts are in machine-readable form (although most of these programs actually produce concordances, with some creative imagination one can make them produce true subject indexes).

Two systems of alphabetizing can be applied to indexes — letter-by-letter and word-by-word. All alphabetizing is, of course, essentially by letter. The letter-by-letter system ignores word spaces and alphabetizes everything up to the first mark of punctuation as if it were all one word; the word-by-word system, in contrast, alphabetizes only up to the first space or mark of punctuation and uses the material that follows only when two first words are identical. The letter-by-letter system is usually preferable. Disregard accent marks in alphabetizing and follow the rules for names given in 2.3.

1.7.6.   Design of books and journals

Although publishers, not authors, are responsible for the design, production, and marketing of books and journals, it is useful for scholars to have some notion of what happens to their manuscripts apart from editing. All books and journals must be designed, no matter how simple and straightforward the result. In selecting page size and typefaces, the designer must consider costs as well as the requirements of the text. The typeface chosen should be capable of conveying the substance of the work in the most legible way (e.g., it may have to have foreign language characters or a letter el that is distinct from the number one), but it should also be economical. Although scholarly publishers are increasingly using "standard" designs for books, each book must be evaluated for its special needs and the appropriateness of a standard design.

One of the first steps in designing a book is "casting off" the manuscript, that is, estimating the number of characters of text. A cleanly prepared manuscript, with consistent margins, greatly facilitates this process, enabling the designer to arrive at a relatively accurate estimate by counting only a few random lines and pages. The character count of a manuscript is then turned into an estimate of the number of pages the book will contain with various typefaces (each gets a different average number of characters in the same space). With these figures the designer can calculate the costs of using various page sizes with various amounts of type on each page. After determining the best combination, the designer writes the specifications. These specifications cover every aspect of the typography of the book, from the size of the indent for each paragraph to the use of embellished type for chapter openings. The following is a portion of the specifications for this book, as designed by Judith Altreuter:

The MLA Style Manual

Composition specifications, third revision

GENERAL

Trim size:	6" x 9"
Margins:	head--1/2"; gutter--3/4"
Type page:	25 x 45 picas
Text page:	25 x 42 picas
Running head:	36 pt. from baseline of running head to baseline of text
	chapter title: 12-pt. Baskerville, centered (same copy left and right)
	section number: 12-pt. Bask. boldface, outside flush
	folio: 10-pt. Bask., inside flush
	No running head on chapter opening pages
Text:	10/12 Bask. x 25 picas
Paragraph indent:	1-em indent
Extract:	9/11 Bask. x 25 picas; 18 pt. b/b above, 24 pt. b/b below to 5 heads or 18 pt. b/b below to text

```
LISTS                 10/12 Bask., 30 pt. b/b above and below
                      entire list

Numbered lists:       2-em indent to number followed by period
                      and then em space to text; numbers to
                      align on the periods. Turnovers to indent
                      to align with first line, no extra space
                      between entries

HEADS

Chapter number:       16-pt. Bask. bold, left flush x 25 picas,
                      em space to ct, align with top of text
                      page

Chapter title (ct):   16/18 Bask. bold caps, TOs align with text
                      of first line, 45 pt. b/b below to h1 or
                      text

Head1 (h1) number:    14-pt. Bask. bold, left flush x 25 picas,
                      em space to h1, 45 pt. b/b above to ct or
                      text
```

The complete specifications, single-spaced, run to three pages and deal with all the intricacies of this book, including the typewriter face used for examples. Scholars interested in the details of book design should consult the references at the end of section 5.9.

The design of a book also includes its jacket and cover, the selection of the paper on which it is to be printed, the cloth or paper with which it will be bound, the method of binding, and the use of headbands in the binding.

Designing a journal involves the same steps, but the designer also has to plan an economical design that is flexible enough to accommodate the editorial plans for the journal and to meet postal and copyright regulations.

1.7.7.   Types of composition processes

Originally typesetting involved selecting preformed metal characters from a case, arranging them into lines on a composing stick, and then, after laying out the lines in galleys to take a proof impression, locking them into chases. The type was then inked and pressed against paper to produce a printed product. The terminology of publishing still reflects these procedures, which held sway for four centuries.

Typesetting was mechanized in the late nineteenth century, with the invention of the Linotype and the Monotype. These machines essentially automated the selection of the metal characters, the Linotype by arranging type matrixes in lines and then casting a solid line of type, the Monotype by casting individual pieces of type in the order needed. Recent decades have seen rapid changes in composition methods, with the result that most books and journals are now composed through some sort of photocomposition system, wherein beams of light formed into the shape of the images to be reproduced (letters, numbers, and symbols) shine on photosensitive paper or film. The beams of light are controlled, ultimately, by a computerized system that records not only the images to be reproduced but also the codes indicating their size and position relative to other images.

Much has been written about the significance of these developments for scholarly publishing, but no two accounts agree. Photocomposition is cheaper or more expensive; corrections are easier or more difficult and prone to additional error; the results match those of the older methods or destroy the art of fine bookmaking. It is helpful for the author in proofreading and in marking proofs to understand the composition process used. Production editors are usually happy to explain the procedure and its significance for the author's role in publishing.

Increasingly, books are being typeset from computer materials supplied by their authors. This procedure requires transforming the writer's computer tape or disk, with its internal codes for producing a manuscript acceptable in appearance to readers and editors, into a tape or disk capable of driving sophisticated typesetting equipment with complex codes of its own. Methods of preparing a manuscript to facilitate this transition are discussed in 3.5.3. Authors working on computers should explore how their word processing systems might satisfy both the most discriminating reader of a manuscript and the needs of a computer system to set type. Careful coding can result in two versions of a tape or disk, identical in substantive content but different in capability, one able to produce a pleasing manuscript and the other readily able to be typeset.

1.7.8. Marketing of books

Since academic libraries and individual scholars are the primary purchasers of scholarly books, publishers do not market them like trade books and textbooks. For academic libraries, reviews, particularly in *Choice*, are extremely important. Publishers attempt to reach individual scholars not only through reviews but also through direct mail, advertisements in scholarly journals, and exhibits at scholarly meetings. Authors can help market their books by providing publishers with lists of journals whose reviews are read and respected by other scholars in the field. For direct-mail advertising of books, publishers rely on lists of their own customers as well as on lists provided by professional and scholarly associations and by several list services. An author can assist in direct-mail advertising by informing the publisher of any special organizations or groups whose members might be particularly interested in the book. Publishers exhibit their books at meetings of major scholarly associations; authors can assist their publishers by directing them to specialized meetings that have exhibit opportunities, but since the costs of exhibiting are quite high, authors should not expect their publishers to exhibit at every meeting.

1.8. Guidelines for author-publisher relations: Summary and conclusion

The relations between authors and publishers should be marked at all times by full and open communication. From this simple premise one can derive specific guidelines for the steps of the publishing process.

An author submitting a prospectus or manuscript for consideration should indicate whether it is being considered elsewhere and whether any part of the proposed work has been or will be published elsewhere. Because of the costs of the evaluation process, many publishers decline to review work being considered elsewhere.

Publishers should acknowledge receipt of a prospectus or manuscript within a reasonable time and let the author know when to expect a decision. Because review procedures vary, it is difficult to define a reasonable time for evaluation. While publishers should complete this step as rapidly as possible, a thorough review of a book-length manuscript can sometimes take more than a year. Should the publisher fail to keep the author informed of the status of the review process, the author can feel free, after giving the publisher reasonable notice, to take the prospectus or manuscript elsewhere.

Following conditional acceptance of a prospectus or manuscript, publishers must indicate to the author exactly what revisions they want. Authors should respond promptly, indicating whether they are willing to make the changes and estimating the date by which the changes will be made.

Once a prospectus or manuscript has been accepted, an author should not attempt to withdraw it, except in extreme circumstances. Most scholarly publishers view the submission of a manuscript as an invitation to publish the manuscript. An author who wishes to place conditions on that invitation should state them clearly when offering the manuscript for consideration.

Throughout the process leading to publication, the author should reply promptly to requests from the publisher and return copyedited manuscript and proofs in accordance with the publisher's schedule. The publisher must keep the author informed of the publishing schedule and allow adequate time for reviewing the copyedited manuscript, correcting proofs, and compiling the index.

An author can often help the publisher promote the book by suggesting journals that are likely to review it and by providing the information the publisher requests. Since most scholarly books are printed in small quantities, the number of copies available for review and promotion purposes is usually limited. Authors can often suggest the best places to send them.

The publisher's contract should spell out all that an author needs to know about the compensation, if any, to be received and the schedule of payments. Authors should read their contracts with care, keeping them available for reference. Since copyrights are personal property that may be assigned in a will or other legal instrument, the contracts relating to published books and articles should be kept among an author's legal papers.

Specific guidelines for the relations between authors and journal editors can be found in *Guidelines for Journal Editors and Contributors*, prepared for the Conference of Editors of Learned Journals (New York: MLA, 1984).

1.9.   Copyright and other legal considerations

In addition to copyright law, the laws that sometimes concern authors deal with libel, invasion of privacy, and occasionally even commerce and trade. It is difficult to generalize in a useful way about the legal considerations surrounding scholarly publishing. This section will point to some that apply within the United States and offer general observations, but there are exceptions and qualifications to almost every possible generalization. Thus an author would be well advised to consult some of the publications listed at the end of this section and, when necessary, to confer with an attorney. Much of the material in this section on copyright is drawn, sometimes verbatim, from Walter S. Achtert, "The New Copyright Law," *PMLA* 93 (1978): 572–77.

1.9.1.   Copyright law

Copyright law in the United States was thoroughly revised by the Copyright Revision Act of 1976, which amended in its entirety section 17 of the United States Code. Most of the new provisions went into effect on 1 January 1978, but some are still being phased in, and the full effect of the law will not be felt until well into the twenty-first century. The major changes that concern scholars and teachers in the humanities are the following: (a) The law established a single system of statutory federal copyright protection for all copyrightable works, whether published or unpublished, abolishing the old dual system of common-law copyright for unpublished works and federal statutory copyright for published works. (b) The term of copyright protection is now the life of the author plus 50 years, for both published and unpublished works. (c) Authors may now reclaim any transfer of rights under copyright after 35 years. (d) The judicial doctrine of "fair use" is part of the statute. (e) The provisions for notice of copyright are more lenient than they were under the old law.

a.   Statutory copyright

The establishment of a single system of limited statutory copyright is the most far-reaching change in the law. Because the transition from the old law to the new one will not be completed for several decades and because the general understanding of copyright law held by scholars is often derived from the old law, it is necessary to consider the changes in some detail. Under the old copyright law, an unpublished work was protected by common-law copyright, retaining for the author and the author's heirs absolute and exclusive rights in perpetuity. Thus permission to quote from or publish any unpublished manuscript had to be obtained, regardless of the age of the manuscript or the extent of the quotation. This provision was both a blessing and a curse for scholars: a blessing because it assured the owners of any unpublished manuscript (and one must always distinguish between the owners of the physical manuscript and the owners of the literary rights to the manuscript) that they could allow scholars to see, read, and even take notes from the manuscript without jeopardizing the value of that property; a curse because it required scholars to search long and hard for the owners of literary rights to any unpublished manuscript before they could quote from or publish the manuscript. Although a scholar could publish the manuscript if the owners of the literary rights could not be discovered after diligent search, there was always the fear that the owners would later surface and sue—and the courts would then have to decide whether the search had been sufficiently diligent. Under the new system of a single federal statutory copyright, unpublished manuscripts are treated the same as published manuscripts: copyright is reserved to the author for a limited time, and the copyright to unpublished works is no longer absolute but subject to statutory exceptions and exemptions. Although the transition provisions of the law (discussed below) keep unpublished manuscripts under copyright protection until at least 2002, the change cannot be emphasized too much: the rights to unpublished works are no longer absolute; such rights are subject to the provisions of fair use and other sections of the copyright law (but the factors involved in judging fair use are likely to be weighed differently for unpublished and published works).

b.   Duration of copyright

Once the new United States copyright law goes completely into effect, it will afford copyright protection to eligible works for a period of the life of the author plus 50 years. This term of protection now covers all works of known personal authorship created after 1 January 1978. For works made for hire (normally written by an author as a salaried employee or, with severe restrictions, under a contract that designates the work as made for hire) and for anonymous and pseudonymous works (unless the identity of the author is recorded in the Copyright Office), the term is 75 years from publication or 100 years from creation, whichever is shorter. Thus, to determine the copyright status of a work, one needs to ascertain that the author is living or when the author died. The Copyright Office maintains records that may be relied on, as a defense in any action for infringement, to establish that an author has died or is still living. In general, the law holds that an author may be presumed dead 75 years after the first publication of a work or 100 years from its creation, unless a record in the Copyright Office testifies otherwise.

A complex series of provisions extends the new law to works existing on 1 January 1978. For works already under statutory federal copyright, the law retains the old term of copyright of 28 years from first publication but allows the copyright to be renewed for a second term of 47 years. To obtain the extended coverage, copyrights subsisting in their first term on 1 January 1978 must be renewed within the last year of their original coverage. Works that were already in their renewal terms or that were legally registered for renewal before 1 January 1978 have had their renewal terms automatically extended to 47 years. A series of acts passed while the revision act was under consideration extended the existing renewal terms of any copyrights that would have expired on or after 19 September 1962, so that they were covered by the new law. Thus, works first copyrighted on 19 September 1906 and duly renewed at the end of 28 years remained under copyright protection until the end of 1981; the copyright on all works published before 1 January 1910 expired at the end of 1984. Works created before 1 January 1978 but neither under statutory copyright before that date nor in the public domain on that date have copyright protection for the life of the author plus 50 years, except that in no instance shall the copyright under this provision expire before 31 December 2002 (and if the work is published before then, copyright shall extend until at least 2027). Thus the copyright to an unpublished manuscript of an author who died, for example, in 1700 will subsist until at least 2002, and if the work is published before the end of 2002, until 2027.

c.   Termination of transfers

An author or certain of an author's heirs may terminate any transfers of rights under copyright after 35 years by serving written notice on the person or corporation to whom the rights were transferred. The written notice must be served within 5 years after the 35 years following the transfer (with some exceptions). Thus, an author may legally abrogate a contract with a publisher after 35 years. The effect of such a termination on the publisher's contracts with others (e.g., for movie rights) is currently the subject of litigation.

For works under copyright either in their original term or in a renewal term on 1 January 1978, transfers of rights under copyright may be terminated within 5 years following 56 years of copyright protection, provided that notice is given at least 2 years, and no more than 10 years, before the effective date of termination.

d. Fair use

United States copyright law now incorporates the doctrine of "fair use" that was originally developed by the courts in exempting certain uses of copyrighted works from charges of infringement. Briefly stated, this doctrine holds that any use of a copyrighted work that is "fair" is not an infringement. One person's concept of "fair," however, is not necessarily another's or the law's. Teachers, for instance, tend to think that any copying they do for their classes is certainly "fair": they have no motive of profit; the copying is not a substitute for the purchase of a book; and the copying of an author's work — even, for example, a long poem — might inspire students to purchase the author's books. But publishers tend to think that no copying is "fair": although teachers may have no motive of profit, copying denies authors their legitimate royalties; if no copying were done, there would be a greater market for anthologies. The entire section of the copyright law dealing with fair use reads as follows:

Notwithstanding the provisions of section 106, the fair use of a copyrighted work, including such use by reproduction in copies or phonorecords or by any other means specified by that section, for purposes such as criticism, comment, news reporting, teaching (including multiple copies for classroom use), scholarship, or research, is not an infringement of copyright. In determining whether the use made of a work in any particular case is a fair use, the factors to be included shall include —

(1) the purpose and character of the use, including whether such use is of a commercial nature or is for nonprofit educational purposes;

(2) the nature of the copyrighted work;

(3) the amount and substantiality of the portion used in relation to the copyrighted work as a whole; and

(4) the effect of the use upon the potential market for or value of the copyrighted work. (17 US Code, sec. 107)

Although these phrases in the law provide some clarification, they leave it to the courts to rule on any particular use. The courts consider these four factors — and any other factors they consider relevant. The "legislative history" of the law provides further guidance on what constitutes fair use, and the courts are free, but not required, to consider it in their deliberations.

The legislative history consists of the committee reports of both houses of Congress, the conference report, and the floor debates that took place before passage of the act. In the legislative history, one finds that Congress attempted to clarify "fair use" in two ways: by stating what changes, if any, it was trying to make in the prevailing legal situation and by providing reasonable "guidelines."

The legislative history is clear about what changes Congress was advocating: none. The Senate and the House committee reports contain the identical sentence: "Section 107 is intended to restate the present judicial doctrine of fair use, not to change, narrow, or enlarge it in any way."

To clarify the law further, Congress "accepted as part" of its "understanding of fair use" a set of "Guidelines for Classroom Copying." These guidelines, about which much has been written, are intended, in the words of the House committee report, to provide "a reasonable interpretation of the *minimum* standards of fair use. Teachers will know that copying within the guidelines is fair use." The guidelines, then, as they themselves state, are minimum and not maximum standards; and, as the committee also pointed out, uses not included within the guidelines might still qualify as fair. The guidelines apply only to copying for one's own use in doing research and in teaching, or preparing to teach, a class; they do not concern fair use in published works. In their entirety, they read as follows:

The purpose of the following guidelines is to state the minimum and not the maximum standards of educational fair use under Section 107 of H.R. 2223. The parties agree that the conditions determining the extent of permissible copying for educational purposes may change in the future; that certain types of copying permitted under these guidelines may not be permissible in the future; and conversely that in the future other types of copying not permitted under these guidelines may be permissible under revised guidelines.

Moreover, the following statement of guidelines is not intended to limit the types of copying permitted under the standards of fair use under judicial decision and which are stated in Section 107 of the Copyright Revision Bill. There may be instances in which copying which does not fall within the guidelines stated below may nonetheless be permitted under the criteria of fair use.

Guidelines

I. *Single Copying for Teachers*

A single copy may be made of any of the following by or for a teacher at his or her individual request for his or her scholarly research or use in teaching or preparation to teach a class:

A. A chapter from a book;

B. An article from a periodical or newspaper;

C. A short story, short essay or short poem, whether or not from a collective work;

D. A chart, graph, diagram, drawing, cartoon or picture from a book, periodical, or newspaper.

II. *Multiple Copies for Classroom Use*

Multiple copies (not to exceed in any event more than one copy per pupil in a course) may be made by or for the teacher giving the course for classroom use or discussion; *provided that:*

A. The copying meets the tests of brevity and spontaneity as defined below; *and,*

B. Meets the cumulative effect test as defined below; *and,*

C. Each copy includes a notice of copyright.

Definitions

Brevity

(i) Poetry: (a) A complete poem if less than 250 words and if printed on not more than two pages or, (b) from a longer poem, an excerpt of not more than 250 words.

(ii) Prose: (a) Either a complete article, story or essay of less than 2,500 words, or (b) an excerpt from any prose work of not more than 1,000 words or 10% of the work, whichever is less, but in any event a minimum of 500 words.

[Each of the numerical limits stated in "i" and "ii" above may be expanded to permit the completion of an unfinished line of a poem or of an unfinished prose paragraph.]

(iii) Illustration: One chart, graph, diagram, drawing, cartoon or picture per book or per periodical issue.

(iv) "Special" works: Certain works in poetry, prose or in "poetic prose" which often combine language with illustrations and which are intended sometimes for children and at other times for a more general audience fall short of 2,500 words in their entirety. Paragraph "ii" above notwithstanding such "special works" may not be reproduced in their entirety; however, an excerpt comprising not more than two of the published pages of such special work and containing not more than 10% of the words found in the text thereof, may be reproduced.

Spontaneity

(i) The copying is at the instance and inspiration of the individual teacher, and

(ii) The inspiration and decision to use the work and the moment of its use for maximum teaching effectiveness are so close in time that it would be unreasonable to expect a timely reply to a request for permission.

Cumulative Effect

(i) The copying of the material is for only one course in the school in which the copies are made.

(ii) Not more than one short poem, article, story, essay or two excerpts may be copied from the same author, nor more than three from the same collective work or periodical volume during one class term.

(iii) There shall not be more than nine instances of such multiple copying for one course during one class term.

[The limitations stated in "ii" and "iii" above shall not apply to current news periodicals and newspapers and current news sections of other periodicals.]

III. *Prohibitions as to I and II Above*

Notwithstanding any of the above, the following shall be prohibited:

(A) Copying shall not be used to create or to replace or substitute for anthologies, compilations or collective works. Such replacement or substitution may occur whether copies of various works or excerpts therefrom are accumulated or reproduced and used separately.

(B) There shall be no copying of or from works intended to be "consumable" in the course of study or of teaching. These include workbooks, exercises, standardized tests and test booklets and answer sheets and like consumable material.

(C) Copying shall not:

(a) Substitute for the purchase of books, publishers' reprints or periodicals;

(b) be directed by higher authority;

(c) be repeated with respect to the same item by the same teacher from term to term.

(D) No charge shall be made to the student beyond the actual cost of the photocopying. (94th Cong., 2nd sess., H. Rept. 94–1476, 68–70)

For photocopying beyond the limits of fair use, publishers have established the Copyright Clearance Center, through which royalties may be paid.

Fair use in scholarly articles and books is a somewhat simpler matter, but scholars who include quotations in their writing should place themselves in the role of the publisher of the work quoted and, considering all four factors listed in the law, judge whether the extracts, either individually or in their cumulative effect, are "fair." If the use does not seem fair, scholars should consult their editors for further guidance. (See 1.9.2 for guidance on how to request permission to use copyrighted work beyond the boundaries of fair use.)

e.   Notice of copyright

The old law provided that, unless every copy of a work (with some exceptions) bore a notice of copyright, the work was in the public domain. One could thus rather readily ascertain whether a work was copyrighted by searching for the notice, which had to be affixed in a prescribed location. The presumptions under the new law are different: statutory copyright now exists from the moment a work is created (and an unpublished work does not need to include a copyright notice to have copyright protection). But published works still require copyright notices. What constitutes publication, however, could be the subject of litigation: to be cautious, scholars should place copyright notices on copies of manuscripts that they circulate widely, such as to persons attending a convention. The new law further provides that within 5 years of publication of a work without notice, action may be taken to secure continued copyright in the work. The effect of all these provisions concerning notice of copyright is that the only way to ascertain whether a published work is copyrighted is to examine the work for a notice of copyright and, if there is none, to search the records of the Copyright Office 5 years after publication.

1.9.2.   Permissions

The use of a copyrighted work beyond that permitted by law requires the consent of the owner of the right to that type of use. The consent given by the owner can be contingent on the payment of a fee, the printing of an acknowledgment in a prescribed wording and location, or any other requirement the owner may wish to set forth. The use of a copyrighted work in a critical article or book is ordinarily within fair use. Scholars should make certain, however, that the "amount and substantiality" of the portion used does not exceed their legitimate needs. Reprinting copyrighted material or quoting from it for its own sake, no matter how brief the excerpt, never constitutes fair use and always requires permission. Thus, for example, publishers cannot publish an anthology of even snippets from reviews of a novel without acquiring the consent of the owners of the rights to those reviews. In any dispute, the courts decide whether a use is fair; they may consider statements by publishers or literary executors that quotation beyond a certain length is not fair use, but such statements do not themselves determine the law. Scholars should ponder the definition of fair use given in the copyright law (see 1.9.1d) and seek permission for uses that do not fall within this definition.

When required, permission must be sought from the owner or the owner's agent. Regardless of the name printed with the copyright notice in a book, the right to reprint passages from the book is most often granted by the publisher (if the publisher does not hold the rights or have the power to act as the agent of the person who does, the publisher can usually direct the request to the appropriate person).

Requests to quote or reprint should be directed to the "Permissions Editor" of the publisher in question and should state clearly the exact material to be quoted or reprinted (including a full citation of the work, the pages on which the material appears, and the opening and closing words) and the manner in which the material will be used (including all details about the intended publication—the name of the publisher, the number of copies to be printed, the audience to which the work is addressed, and its price). Since many publishers, particularly publishers of journals, routinely seek the author's consent before granting permission to reprint an essay, scholars should allow at least six weeks to receive a response.

1.9.3.   Libel and other legal considerations

The laws defining "libel" are as complex as any other body of law. Generally speaking, a written statement that unjustly damages a person's reputation is libelous. Likewise, scholars should be aware, laws protecting the right of privacy are sometimes invoked against authors. Scholars who feel that what they have written might damage the reputation of a person (living or dead) or might reveal private matters about a person should confer with their publishers about this possibility or else consult their own attorneys.

1.9.4. Further guidance

Further guidance in these matters can be sought in the works listed below:

Publications of the Copyright Office

The publications of the Copyright Office are, of course, authoritative, but the Copyright Office is prohibited from providing any interpretation of the law except in the form of regulations. The following publications are available free of charge from the Copyright Office (Library of Congress, Washington, DC 20559):

Copyright and the Librarian. Circular R21. 9 pp.
Duration of Copyright under the New Law. Circular R15a. 3 pp.
Extension of Copyright Term in Certain Cases under Copyright Act of 1976. Circular R15t. 2 pp.
Highlights of the New Copyright Law. Circular R99. 4 pp.
Public Law 94–553 (90 Stat. 2541). 62 pp. [The copyright law itself.]
Reproduction of Copyrighted Works by Educators and Librarians. Circular R21. 26 pp.

Other publications

The publications listed below often provide more helpful guidance, since their authors are not prohibited from expressing opinions and offering interpretations. A number of articles, pamphlets, and books have been excluded from this list because they overstate the restrictions on fair use.

Copyright Revision Act of 1976: Law, Explanation, Committee Reports. Chicago: Commerce Clearing House, 1976. 279 pp.

Johnston, Donald F. *Copyright Handbook.* 2nd ed. New York: Bowker, 1982. 381 pp.

The New Copyright Law: Questions Teachers and Librarians Ask. Washington: Natl. Educ. Assn., 1977. 76 pp.

Spilhaus, A. F., Jr. "The Copyright Clearance Center." *Scholarly Publishing* 9 (1978): 143–48.

Thorpe, James. *The Use of Manuscripts in Literary Research: Problems of Access and Literary Property Rights.* 2nd ed. New York: MLA, 1979. 40 pp.

2 MECHANICS OF WRITING

Although the scope of this book precludes a detailed discussion of grammar, usage, readability, and related concerns in scholarly writing, this chapter addresses questions that commonly arise about the mechanical aspects of style:

1. Spelling
2. Punctuation
3. Names of persons
4. Capitalization
5. Titles in manuscripts
6. Quotations
7. Numbers
8. Transliteration

For more comprehensive discussions of these matters, see the standard handbooks of writing, such as those listed in 1.3.

2.1. Spelling

2.1.1. Consistency and "preferred" spelling

Spelling, including hyphenation, should be consistent throughout the manuscript—except in quotations, which must retain the spelling of the sources.

To ensure accuracy and consistency, always use a single widely recognized authority for spelling; most publishers recommend *Webster's Collegiate Dictionary* or, if the word is not listed there, *Webster's Third New International Dictionary*. Where entries show variant spellings, use the form given first or, if the variants have separate listings, the form that appears with the full definition. Inform your editor, before copyediting begins, of any necessary deviations from this practice.

2.1.2. Word division

Avoid dividing a word at the end of a line. Leave the line short—even extremely short—rather than divide a word.

2.1.3.   Accents

In quoting, reproduce all accents exactly as they appear in the original. If your typewriter does not have accent marks, write them in by hand.

In French, an accented letter does not always retain the accent mark when capitalized (the accent required in *école* may be omitted in *Ecole*, for example), but an accent is never unacceptable over a capital letter that would require one if it were lowercase. When transcribing words that appear in all capitals and changing them to lowercase (as in transcribing a title from a title page), insert the necessary accents.

2.1.4.   Diaeresis

In German words the diaeresis, not *e*, should be used for the umlaut (*ä, ö, ü* rather than *ae, oe, ue*), even for initial capitals (*Über*). But common usage must be observed for names: Götz, *but* Goethe. Alphabetize words with the diaeresis without regard to the diaeresis.

2.1.5.   Digraphs

A digraph is a combination of two letters that represents only one sound (e.g., *th, oa* in *broad*). In many languages, some digraphs appear united in print (*æ, œ, ß*); transcribe them in typescript without any connection between them (*ae, oe, ss*). (If it is necessary to reproduce the united character as closely as possible, write in the character or join the tops of the two typed letters.)

In American English, the digraph *ae* is being abandoned in favor of *e* alone: *archeology, encyclopedia,* and *medieval* are now common spellings. Follow the dictionary you have adopted for your work.

2.1.6.   Plurals

The plurals of English words are generally formed by adding the suffix *-s* or *-es*. The tendency in American English is to form the plurals of words naturalized from other languages in the same manner. The plurals *libretti* and *formulae*, for example, are giving way to *librettos* and *formulas*. But other adopted words, like *alumni* and *phenomena*, retain the original plurals. Consult a dictionary for guidance. (See 2.2.2 for plurals of letters and for possessive forms of plurals.)

2.2.   Punctuation

2.2.1.   Consistency

The primary purpose of punctuation is to ensure the clarity and readability of writing. Although punctuation is, to some extent, a matter of personal preference, there are many required uses, and while certain practices are optional, consistency is mandatory. Writers must guard against using different punctuation in parallel situations within the same work. Likewise, editors of journals and of essay collections must adopt a "house style" to avoid confusing readers by presenting divergent practices within a single publication.

2.2.2.   Apostrophes

Apostrophes indicate contractions and possessives. To form the possessive of a singular noun, add an apostrophe and an *s* (the accountant's ledger, television's influence); to form the possessive of a plural noun ending in *s*, add only an apostrophe (the accountants' ledgers, the soldiers' weapons). Some irregular plurals require an apostrophe and an *s* (the media's role, women's studies). All singular proper nouns, including the names of persons and places, form their possessives in the same manner (Mars's wrath, Camus's novel, Kansas's weather, Dickens's popularity, *but* the Dickenses' economic problems).

Also use apostrophes to form the plurals of letters (*p*'s and *q*'s; *A*'s, *B*'s, *C*'s). But do not use apostrophes to form the plurals of abbreviations or numbers (PhDs, MAs, 1960s, fours, 780s, SATs in the 780s).

2.2.3.   Colons

A colon introduces an example, explanation, or elaboration of what has just been said. Do not use a colon where a semicolon is appropriate (see 2.2.13).

```
Foucault's warning reminds us of something no historian of

ideas should forget: terms like microcosm and organic have

different meanings in different historical contexts.
```

but

Foucault's warning reminds us of something no historian of

ideas should forget; the historian who does forget looks at

the past through distorting lenses.

Colons are commonly used to introduce quotations (see 2.6.2–3) and to separate titles from subtitles (*Anatomy of Criticism: Four Essays*).

In references and bibliographic citations, colons separate volume numbers from page numbers (3: 81–112), the city of publication from the name of the book publisher (New York: Norton, 1983), and the date of publication from the page numbers of an article in a periodical (15 Feb. 1980: 10–15). Skip only one space after a colon, never two.

2.2.4.   Commas

Commas are required between items in a series, between coordinate adjectives, before coordinating conjunctions joining independent clauses, around parenthetical elements, and after fairly long phrases or clauses preceding the main clauses of sentences.

The experience demanded blood, sweat, and tears.

Vivid, macabre images characterize her early poetry.

Congress passed the bill by a wide margin, and the president

signed it into law.

The invention, the first in a series during that decade,

completely changed people's lives.

After carefully studying all the available historical

```
documents and personal writings, scholars could come to no

definitive conclusion.
```

Commas are also used in dates (March 23, 1986; *but* 23 March 1986), names (D. W. Robertson, Jr., and Walter J. Ong, SJ; *but* John R. Hayes III), and addresses (32 Lexington Avenue, New York, New York, and 2 Park Place, Boston, Massachusetts). If you need a dash where the context would ordinarily require a comma—as you do here—omit the comma. Never use a comma and a dash together. If the context requires a comma after words enclosed in parentheses (as it does here), the comma follows the closing parenthesis. (See 2.6.6 for commas with quotations; see chs. 4 and 5 for the many uses of the comma in documentation and bibliography.)

2.2.5. Dashes

To indicate a dash, type two hyphens, leaving no space before, between, or after. Do not overuse dashes, substituting them for other punctuation marks. Dashes may surround a parenthetical element that represents a sharp break in the flow of thought or that requires internal commas, and a dash should introduce a summarizing appositive.

```
The rapid spread of the disease--the number of reported cases

doubled each six months--helped create the sense of panic.
```

```
Many twentieth-century American writers--Capote, Faulkner,

Styron, Welty, to name only a few--come from the South.
```

```
Computer chips, integrated circuits, bits, and bytes--these

new terms baffled yet intrigued.
```

2.2.6. Exclamation marks

Except in direct quotation, avoid using exclamation marks in scholarly writing.

2.2.7.   Hyphens

Use hyphens to connect numbers indicating a range (1–20) and to form some types of compound words, primarily combinations that function as attributive adjectives (a well-established policy, a first-rate study). Also use hyphens between prefixes and capitalized words (post-Renaissance) and between pairs of coequal nouns (poet-priest, scholar-athlete). Many other word combinations, however, are written as one word (hardworking employees, storytelling) or as two or more words (social security tax, ad hoc committee); adverbs ending in "ly" do not form hyphenated compounds (a wildly successful debut). Consult a standard dictionary (see 2.1.1) for guidance on the hyphenation of specific terms.

In documentation, a hyphen links the name of a publisher's imprint and the name of the publisher (Anchor-Doubleday).

2.2.8.   Italics

Represent italics by underlining, not by "script" or other fancy typewriter faces. Use codes, as described in 3.5.3, if your typewriter or word processor will not conveniently underline.

Some titles are italicized (see 2.5.2), as are letters, words, or phrases cited as linguistic examples, words referred to as words, and foreign words in an English text. The numerous exceptions to this last rule include quotations entirely in another language; non-English titles of short works (poems, short stories, essays, articles), which are placed in quotation marks and not underlined; proper names; and foreign words anglicized through frequent use. Since American English rapidly naturalizes words, use a dictionary to decide whether a foreign expression requires italics. Adopted foreign words, abbreviations, and phrases commonly not underlined include cliché, détente, e.g., et al., etc., genre, hubris, laissez-faire, leitmotiv, mimesis, raison d'être, roman à clef, tête-à-tête, and versus.

Avoid using italics for emphasis, since this device rapidly loses its effectiveness.

2.2.9.   Parentheses

Parentheses, like dashes, enclose parenthetical remarks that break too sharply with the surrounding text to be enclosed in commas. Parentheses sometimes dictate a greater separation than dashes would, but often either set of marks is acceptable, the choice depending on the other punctuation required in the context. Parentheses are used around documentation within the text (see 5.2) and around publication information in notes (see 5.8.3).

2.2.10. Periods

Periods end declarative sentences, notes, and complete blocks of information in bibliographic citations. Periods between numbers indicate related parts of a work (e.g., 1.2 for act 1, scene 2).

The period follows a parenthesis incorporated at the end of a sentence. It goes within the parenthesis when the enclosed element is independent (see, not this sentence, but the next). (For the use of periods with ellipsis points, see 2.6.4.)

2.2.11. Question marks

Question marks end interrogatory sentences and, in the list of works cited, indicate uncertainty about the accuracy of information supplied in square brackets but not stated in the source: [1983?]. (See 4.5.25 for listing books that do not state publication information.)

2.2.12. Quotation marks

Quotation marks enclose quoted material (see 2.6), certain titles (see 2.5.3), and words or phrases purposely misused or used in a special sense (e.g., their "benefactor" was ultimately responsible for their downfall).

Use double quotation marks around translations of words or phrases from another language or around definitions of words when the translation or definition is parenthetical (that is, separated from the word defined or translated by commas or parentheses). Use single quotation marks for definitions or translations that appear without intervening punctuation (*ainsi* 'thus').

2.2.13. Semicolons

Semicolons separate items in series when some of the items require internal commas. They also connect closely related independent clauses not joined by coordinating conjunctions and precede coordinating conjunctions linking independent clauses that require a number of internal commas.

```
In one day the indefatigable candidate campaigned in Vail,

Colorado; Columbus, Ohio; Nashville, Tennessee; and Teaneck,

New Jersey.
```

```
On the one hand, demand is steadily decreasing; on the other,

production keeps inexplicably increasing.
```

```
The overture begins with a brooding, mournful passage in the

strings and woodwinds, one of the composer's most passionate

statements; but the piece concludes with a burst of lively,

spirited, almost comic music in the brass and percussion.
```

In bibliography and documentation, use semicolons to separate multiple publishers of a book (4.5.20) and two or more works in a single parenthetical reference (5.5.9) or in a single bibliographic note (5.6.2). In documentation notes, use them in citing republished books (5.8.5k) and serialized articles (5.8.6m).

2.2.14. Slashes

Slashes (or virgules) separate lines of poetry, elements in dates expressed exclusively in digits (e.g., 2/12/84), and, occasionally, alternative words (and/or). Use a space before and after the slash only when separating lines of poetry (see 2.6.3).

2.2.15. Square brackets

Square brackets replace parentheses within parentheses and enclose interpolations in quotations (see 2.6.5). In documentation, they enclose English names of foreign cities (4.5.22), translations of titles in languages other than English (4.5.22), and interpolations of data not supplied by the sources cited (see 4.5.25). Insert square brackets by hand if they are not on your typewriter.

2.2.16. Multiple punctuation

Where the rules of punctuation would call for two or more marks of punctuation to fall in the same location or next to one another, you should generally retain only the strongest mark. Although any ranking of punctuation marks in order of strength is open to exceptions, the ordinary progression from weakest to strongest is comma, semicolon, colon, dash, period, question mark, exclamation mark. But always retain a period indicating an abbreviation unless the period coincides with another period: Is that Thomas Brown, Sr.? *but* It is Thomas Brown, Sr. Other marks of punctuation can fall next to quotation marks and, in some instances, parentheses, brackets, and dashes. But never use commas and dashes together or put a comma before a parenthesis or a bracket.

Parentheses, quotation marks, and brackets supplement other punctuation. Parentheses and brackets take logical positions in relation to other punctuation marks. By convention, a closing single or double quotation mark always follows a period or comma even if it should logically precede. Quotation marks take logical positions relative to other marks of punctuation. (See 2.2.4 for commas and dashes, 2.2.10 for periods and parentheses, and 2.6.6 for punctuation with quotation marks.)

2.3. Names of persons

2.3.1. First and subsequent uses of names

Except in referring casually to the very famous—say, Mozart or Shakespeare—state a person's name in full the first time it appears in your manuscript.

```
Arthur George Rust, Jr.

Victoria M. Sackville-West
```

In subsequent uses of the name, give the person's last name only (Sackville-West)—unless, of course, you refer to two or more persons with the same last name—or give the most common form of the person's name (e.g., Michelangelo for Michelangelo Buonarroti; Surrey for Henry Howard, earl of Surrey; Disraeli for Benjamin Disraeli, first earl of Beaconsfield). In some languages (e.g., Chinese, Hungarian, Japanese, Korean, and Vietnamese), surnames precede given names (see 2.3.7 and 2.3.12).

2.3.2. Titles of persons

In general, do not use formal titles (Dr., Father, Miss, Mr., Mrs., Ms., Professor, Sister, etc., or their equivalents in other languages) in referring to persons, living or dead: Churchill, *not* Mr. Churchill; Dickinson, *not* Miss Dickinson; Mead, *not* Professor Mead; Stowe, *not* Mrs. Stowe. Retain the titles traditionally used with a few famous women (e.g., Mrs. Humphry Ward, Mme de Staël).

2.3.3. Names of authors and fictional characters

It is common and acceptable to use simplified names of famous authors (Vergil for Publius Vergilius Maro, Dante for Dante Alighieri). Treat pseudonyms like ordinary names.

> Molière (Jean-Baptiste Poquelin)
> Voltaire (François-Marie Arouet)
> George Sand (Amandine-Aurore-Lucie Dupin)
> George Eliot (Mary Ann Evans)
> Mark Twain (Samuel Clemens)
> Stendhal (Marie-Henri Beyle)
> Novalis (Friedrich von Hardenberg)

Refer to fictional characters as they are referred to in the text. You need not always use last names (e.g., Tom, for Tom Jones) and you may retain titles (e.g., Dr. Jekyll).

2.3.4. Dutch and German names

Dutch *van*, *van der*, and *van den* and German *von* are generally not used with the last name alone, but there are some exceptions, especially in English contexts, where the *van* or *von* is firmly established by convention.

Beethoven, Ludwig van
Droste-Hülshoff, Annette von
Kleist, Heinrich von
Vondel, Joost van den

but

Van Gogh, Vincent
Von Braun, Wernher

Alphabetize German names with umlauts indicated by diaeresis (ä, ö, ü) without regard to the diaeresis. Do not, for example, convert ü to ue.

2.3.5. French names

With some exceptions, French *de* following a given name or a title such as *Mme* or *duc* is not used with the last name alone and is not capitalized:

La Boétie, Etienne de
La Bruyère, Jean de
Maupassant, Guy de
Nemours, duc de
Ronsard, Pierre de
Scudéry, Madeleine de

When the last name has only one syllable, however, *de* is usually retained:

de Gaulle, Charles

The preposition also remains, in the form *d'*, when it elides with a last name beginning with a vowel:

d'Arcy, Pierre
d'Arsonval, Arsène

Similarly the forms *du* and *des* — combinations of *de* with a following *le* or *les* — are always used with last names:

Des Périers, Bonaventure
Du Bartas, Guillaume de Salluste

A hyphen is normally used between French given names (M.-J. Chénier is Marie-Joseph Chénier, *but* M. R. Char is Monsieur René Char, P. J. Reynard is Père J. Reynard).

2.3.6. Greek names

In Greek books, the author's name appears on the title page in the genitive case (Hypo ["by"] Perikleous Alexandrou Argyropoulou). The first name and usually the surname of a man are nominative (some surnames, however, are always genitive). The second, or patronymic, remains genitive because it means "son of" (Periklēs Alexandrou Argyropoulos). The first name of a woman is nominative, the patronymic and surname both genitive (Aikaterinē Geōrgiou Koumarianou).

On transliterating Greek, see 2.8.

2.3.7. Hungarian names

In Hungarian, the surname precedes the given name:

Bartók Béla
Bessenyei György
Illyés Gyula
Molnár Ferenc
Nagy László
Szabó Magda

In English texts, Hungarian names usually appear with the given name first and the surname last:

Béla Bartók
György Bessenyei
Gyula Illyés
Ferenc Molnár
László Nagy
Magda Szabó

2.3.8.　Italian names

The names of many Italians who lived before or during the Renaissance are alphabetized by first name.

> Bonvesin de la Riva
> Cino da Pistoia
> Dante Alighieri
> Iacopone da Todi
> Michelangelo Buonarroti

But other names of the period follow the standard practice.

> Boccaccio, Giovanni
> Cellini, Benvenuto
> Stampa, Gaspara

The names of members of historic families are also usually alphabetized by last name.

> Este, Beatrice d'
> Medici, Lorenzo de'

The Italian *da, de, del, della,* and *di* are used with the last names of persons from the modern era. The particle is usually capitalized and treated as an integral part of the name, even though a space may separate it from the nominal portion.

> D'Annunzio, Gabriele
> De Sanctis, Francesco
> Del Buono, Oreste
> Della Casa, Giovanni
> Di Costanzo, Angelo

2.3.9.　Russian names

See J. Thomas Shaw, *The Transliteration of Modern Russian for English-Language Publications* (1967; New York: MLA, 1979), for a more extended discussion of which system of transliteration to use for Russian names in various circumstances and when to use common Western forms of names. The following is adopted from Shaw.

Russian names have three parts: prenames, patronymics, and surnames. Prenames of Russians should be transliterated according to the appropriate system rather than given in their English equivalents (e.g., Ivan, *not* John). The only exception is the prename of a Russian ruler used alone (without the patronymic); in this case, use the English equivalent (Michael I, *but* Mikhail Pavlovich).

The form of patronymics in Russian varies by gender, as the form of surnames often does. For example, Aleksandr Sergeevich Pushkin was the husband of Natal'ia Nikolaevna Pushkina. The treatment of such names in an English text will depend on the audience, the predominance of masculine or feminine names in the text, and particularly on whether the text uses names without prenames. In general, the feminine forms should be used for the feminine names and the masculine forms for the masculine names. On occasion, however, particularly in a casual reference to Russians in a work not on Russian studies, some modifications may be acceptable. Scholars not familiar with Russian names must exercise care in balancing accuracy with clarity.

2.3.10. Spanish names

Spanish *de* is not used before the last name alone.

> Las Casas, Bartolomé de
> Madariaga, Salvador de
> Rueda, Lope de
> Timoneda, Juan de

Spanish *del*, formed from the fusion of the preposition *de* and the definite article *el*, must be used with the last name: Del Río, Angel.

Spanish surnames often include both the paternal name and the maternal name, with or without the conjunction *y*. The surname of a married woman usually includes her paternal surname and the paternal surname of the husband, connected by *de*. To index Spanish names properly, you have to distinguish between given names and surnames (your sources or a biographical dictionary can provide guidance). Alphabetize by paternal name.

Álvarez, Miguel de los Santos
Cervantes Saavedra, Miguel de
Díaz de Castillo, Bernal
Figuera Aymerich, Ángela
Larra y Sánchez de Castro, Mariano José
López de Ayala, Pero
Matute, Ana María
Ortega y Gasset, José
Quevedo y Villegas, Francisco Gómez de
Sinues de Marco, María del Pilar
Zayas y Sotomayor, María de

Even persons commonly known by the maternal portions of their surnames — Galdós, Lorca — should be indexed under their full surnames:

García Lorca, Federico
Pérez Galdós, Benito

2.3.11. Latin names

In classical times, Roman male citizens generally had three names: praenomen (given name), nomen (clan name), and cognomen (family or familiar name). Men in this category are usually referred to by nomen, cognomen, or both; your source or a standard reference book such as the *Oxford Classical Dictionary* will provide guidance.

Brutus (Marcus Iunius Brutus)
Calpurnius Siculus (Titus Calpurnius Siculus)
Cicero (Marcus Tullius Cicero)
Lucretius (Titus Lucretius Carus)
Plautus (Titus Maccius Plautus)

Roman women usually had two names: nomen (the clan name in the feminine form) and cognomen (often derived from the father's cognomen): Livia Drusilla (daughter of Marcus Livius Drusus). Sometimes a woman's cognomen indicated her chronological order among the daughters of the family: Antonia Minor (younger daughter of Marcus Antonius). Most Roman women are referred to by nomen: Calpurnia, Clodia, Octavia,

Sulpicia. Some, however, are better known by cognomen: Agrippina (Vip-
sania Agrippina).
When citing Roman names, use the forms most common in English:

> Horace (Quintus Horatius Flaccus)
> Julius Caesar (Gaius Iulius Caesar)
> Juvenal (Decimus Iunius Iuvenalis)
> Livy (Titus Livius)
> Ovid (Publius Ovidius Naso)
> Quintilian (Marcus Fabius Quintilianus)
> Terence (Publius Terentius Afer)
> Vergil (Publius Vergilius Maro)

Finally, some medieval and Renaissance figures are best known by their
adopted or assigned Latin names:

> Albertus Magnus (Albert von Bollstädt)
> Comenius (Jan Amos Komenský)
> Copernicus (Niklas Koppernigk)
> Paracelsus (Theophrastus Bombast von Hohenheim)

2.3.12. Oriental names

In Chinese, Japanese, Korean, and Vietnamese, surnames precede
given names (Hu Shih, Wang Kuowei, Kim Jong Gil, Anesaki Masaharu),
but Western authors should follow the known preferences of Oriental persons, even if these forms do not accord with normal practice or standard
romanization (Y. R. Chao, Syngman Rhee).
The introduction of the pinyin system of romanization for Chinese creates problems in the romanization of Chinese names. In scholarly writing, you will have to balance the sometimes conflicting goals of consistency
and clarity for your audience. In general, use the pinyin spelling for the
names of all persons but add the modified Wade-Giles spelling, in parentheses, for the names of persons who died before 1950. This practice will
allow persons unfamiliar with the systems of romanization to become familiar with the differences and to locate information in other scholarly
works.

2.3.13. Names in other languages

For the names of persons in a language with which you are not familiar, consult reference works or scholars in the language for guidance on the order of names and the use of prefixes (as in Arabic names).

In bibliographic entries for works that include a transliteration of the author's name on the title page, cite the author's name according to the appropriate system of transliteration (see 2.8), followed by the transliteration printed on the title page (in parentheses).

2.4. Capitalization

2.4.1. English

The increasing tendency in English is to use lowercase letters whenever possible. Always capitalize, however, the first word of a sentence, the subject pronoun *I*, the names and initials of persons (except for some particles), proper names, names of days and months, and titles that immediately precede names (but not titles used alone: e.g., the president, a professor of English).

In both titles and subtitles of works (such as novels or essays) and of divisions of works (such as chapters), capitalize the first words, the last words (even if a subtitle follows), and all the principal words, including those that follow hyphens in compound terms. That is, capitalize nouns, pronouns, verbs, adjectives, and adverbs but not articles, prepositions introducing phrases, coordinating conjunctions, or the *to* in infinitives, when such words fall in the middle of the title. Follow this style even if the capitalization differs from that used in the work cited. Unless the title itself has ending punctuation, use a colon and a space to separate a title and a subtitle. Include other punctuation only if it is part of the title.

Death of a Salesman

The Teaching of Spanish in English-Speaking Countries

Storytelling and Mythmaking: Images from Film and Literature

What Is Literature?

Whose Music? A Sociology of Musical Language

<u>Where Did You Go? Out. What Did You Do? Nothing.</u>

"Ode to a Nightingale"

"Italian Literature before Dante"

"What Americans Stand For: Two Views"

"Why Fortinbras?"

When the first line of a poem serves as the title or part of the title, however, reproduce the line exactly as it appears in print ("Not marble, nor the gilded monuments").

In the name of a magazine or newspaper, an initial definite article is usually not treated as part of the title (the *Washington Post*). Capitalize the word *series* or *edition* only when it is part of a title (the Norton Critical Edition, the Twayne World Authors Series, *but* Penguin edition, the Studies in English Literature series). Do not capitalize the general name for a part of a work — for example, preface, introduction, or appendix — unless it is a well-known title, such as Wordsworth's Preface to *Lyrical Ballads*. Capitalize the divisions of works in notes and bibliographies only when they follow periods.

Do not capitalize a noun — or, in documentation, its abbreviation — followed by a numeral indicating place in a sequence: vol. 2 of 3 vols., pl. 4, no. 20, act 5, ch. 3, version A. Never capitalize entire words (i.e., every letter) in titles cited in text or bibliographies (even if the words are capitalized on the title page), except, of course, for the titles of journals that are composed of initials (e.g., *PMLA*).

2.4.2. French

Apart from titles, French usage follows English except that the following terms are not capitalized unless they begin sentences or, sometimes, lines of verse: (1) the subject pronoun *je* 'I,' (2) days and months, (3) languages and the adjectives derived from proper nouns, and (4) titles preceding personal names and the words for street, square, and similar places.

Un Français m'a parlé anglais place de la Concorde.

Hier j'ai vu le docteur Maurois qui conduisait une voiture Ford.

```
Le capitaine Boutillier m'a dit qu'il partait pour Rouen le

premier jeudi d'avril avec quelques amis normands.
```

In both titles and subtitles, capitalize only the first words and all words normally capitalized.

```
Du côté de chez Swann

Le grand Meaulnes

La guerre de Troie n'aura pas lieu

Nouvelle revue des deux mondes

L'ami du peuple
```

Some editors, however, follow other rules. When the title of a work begins with an article, they also capitalize the first noun and any preceding adjectives. In titles of series and periodicals, they capitalize all major words.

2.4.3. German

Apart from titles, German usage follows English, with some important exceptions. Always capitalized in German are (1) all substantives, including any adjectives, infinitives, pronouns, prepositions, or other parts of speech used as substantives, and (2) the pronoun *Sie* 'you' and its possessive *Ihr* 'your' and their inflected forms. Not capitalized unless they begin sentences or, usually, lines of verse are (1) the subject pronoun *ich* 'I,' (2) when used as adjectives or adverbs, days of the week or names of languages, and (3) adjectives and adverbs formed from proper nouns, except when they refer explicitly to the works or deeds of the persons from whose names they are derived.

```
Ich glaube an das Gute in der Welt.
```

```
Er schreibt, nur um dem Auf und Ab der Buch-Nachfrage zu

entsprechen.
```

Fahren Sie mit Ihrer Frau zurück?

Ein französischer Schriftsteller, den ich gut kenne, arbeitet

sonntags immer an seinem neuen Buch über die platonische

Liebe.

Der Staat ist eine der bekanntesten Platonischen Schriften.

In letters and ceremonial writings, the pronouns *du* 'you' and *ihr* 'your' and their derivatives are capitalized.

In titles and subtitles, capitalize the first words and all words normally capitalized.

Ein treuer Diener seines Herrn

Zeitschrift für vergleichende Sprachforschung

"Die Wölfe kommen zurück"

2.4.4. Italian

Apart from titles, Italian usage follows English except that the following terms are not capitalized unless they begin sentences or, usually, lines of verse: (1) the subject pronoun *io* 'I,' (2) days and months, (3) languages, (4) nouns, adjectives, and adverbs derived from proper nouns, and (5) titles preceding personal names and the words for street, square, and similar places. But centuries and other large divisions of time are capitalized.

Un italiano parlava francese con uno svizzero in piazza di

Spagna.

Il dottor Bruno ritornerà dall'Italia giovedì otto agosto e io

partirò il nove.

```
la lirica del Novecento

il Rinascimento
```

In both titles and subtitles, capitalize only the first words and all words normally capitalized.

```
Dizionario letterario Bompiani

Bibliografia della critica pirandelliana

L'arte tipografica in Urbino

Collezione di classici italiani

Studi petrarcheschi
```

2.4.5. Portuguese

Apart from titles, Portuguese usage follows English except that the following terms are not capitalized unless they begin sentences or, usually, lines of verse: (1) the subject pronoun *eu* 'I,' (2) days of the week, (3) months in Brazil (they are capitalized in Portugal), (4) adjectives derived from proper nouns, and (5) titles preceding personal names and the words for street, square, and similar places in Portugal (they are capitalized in Brazil). As in English, points of the compass are not capitalized when indicating direction (ao norte da América) but are capitalized when indicating regions (os americanos do Norte). Brazilian Portuguese capitalizes nouns used to refer to abstract concepts, to institutions, or to branches of knowledge (a Igreja, a Nação, a Matemática).

Peninsular usage

```
Vi o doutor Silva na praça da República.
```

Brazilian usage

```
O francês falava da História do Brasil na Praça Tiradentes,

utilizando o inglês.
```

Ontem eu vi o Doutor Gracia, aquêle que tem um carro Ford.

Então me disse Dona Teresa que pretendia sair para o Recife
a primeira segunda-feira de abril com alguns amigos mineiros.

In both titles and subtitles, capitalize only the first words and all words
normally capitalized.

O bico da pena

O espírito das leis

Problemas da linguagem e do estilo

Boletim de filologia

Revista lusitana

Correio da manhã

Some scholars, however, capitalize all major words.

As Viagens do Infante Dom Pedro às Quatro Partes do Mundo

Gabriela, Cravo e Canela

2.4.6.   Russian

Apart from titles, Russian usage follows English except that the following terms are not capitalized unless they begin sentences or, usually,
lines of verse: (1) the subject pronoun *ja* 'I', (2) days and months, (3) languages and the adjectives derived from proper nouns, and (4) titles preceding personal names and the words for street, square, and similar places.
Transliterated Russian should follow the same usage.

V subbotu, trinadcatogo aprelja, prazdnuja svoj den'

roždenija, doktor Petuxov vnov' vspomnil o svoej

vstreče s francuzom iz Liona na ulice Marata.

V to vremja peterburgskaja znat' predpočitala govorit' po-
francuzski.

Naprasno ia pytalsja ugovorit' ego ne delat' ètogo.

In both titles and subtitles and in the names of organizations and institutions, capitalize the first words and all words normally capitalized.

"K istorii obrazovanija vostočnoslavjanskix jazykov: Po

dannym Galickogo evangelija 1266-1301 gg."

Follow the same usage for titles of series and periodicals.

Obščestvennye nauki za rubežom: Literaturovedenie

Voprosy jazykoznanija

2.4.7. Spanish

Apart from titles, Spanish usage follows English except that the following terms are not capitalized unless they begin sentences or, sometimes, lines of verse: (1) the subject pronoun *yo* 'I,' (2) days and months,
(3) nouns or adjectives derived from proper nouns, (4) titles preceding
personal names and the words for street, square, and similar places.

El francés hablaba inglés en la plaza Colón.

Ayer yo vi al doctor García, que manejaba un coche Ford.

Me dijo don Jorge que iba a salir para Sevilla el primer

martes de abril con unos amigos neoyorkinos.

In both titles and subtitles, capitalize only the first words and words normally capitalized.

Historia verdadera de la conquista de la Nueva España

La gloria de don Ramiro

Extremos de América

Trasmundo de Goya

Breve historia del ensayo hispanoamericano

Revista de filología española

2.4.8. Latin

Although practice varies, Latin most commonly follows the English rules for capitalization, except that *ego* 'I' is not capitalized.

Semper ego auditor tantum? Numquamne reponam / Vexatus totiens

rauci Theseide Cordi?

Quidquid id est, timeo Danaos et dona ferentes.

Nil desperandum.

Quo usque tandem abutere, Catilina, patientia nostra?

In both titles and subtitles, however, capitalize only the first words and words normally capitalized.

De senectute

Liber de senectute

Medievalia et humanistica

2.4.9. Other languages

In transliterating or romanizing languages that do not have capital letters (e.g., Arabic, Chinese, Japanese), capitalize the first words of sentences or, usually, of lines of poetry and all names of persons and places. In Arabic, the article *al* (and its forms) is lowercase in all positions except when it begins a sentence. The same rules apply to words from these languages used as foreign words in the text (and thus underlined). Transliterated names of institutions, religions, movements, and the like should be capitalized in accordance with English usage when these words are not treated as foreign words in the text (i.e., when they are not underlined within an English sentence). In both titles and subtitles, capitalize only the first words and all names of persons and places.

The Chicago Manual of Style, Georg F. von Ostermann, *Manual of Foreign Languages*, the United States Government Printing Office *Style Manual*, and *Words into Type* contain additional information on capitalization in a variety of languages (see 5.9).

2.5. Titles in manuscripts

2.5.1. General guidelines

Always take the title from the title page, not from the cover or from the top of each page. Do not reproduce any unusual typographical characteristics, such as all capital letters or the uncommon use of lowercase letters: MODERNISM & NEGRITUDE should appear as *Modernism and Negritude*; **BERNARD BERENSON** The Making of a Connoisseur as *Bernard Berenson: The Making of a Connoisseur*; Turner's early sketchbooks as *Turner's Early Sketchbooks*.

To indicate titles in the text, whether in English or another language, either underline them or enclose them in quotation marks. In general, underline the titles of works published independently and use quotation marks for the titles of works published within larger works.

2.5.2. Underlined titles

Underline the names of books, plays, long poems published as books, pamphlets, periodicals (newspapers, magazines, and journals), films, radio and television programs, record albums, ballets, operas, instrumental musical compositions (except those identified simply by form, number, and key), paintings, works of sculpture, and ships, aircraft, and spacecraft. Typing a continuous line is easier than breaking for the spaces, and it guards against the error of failing to underline the punctuation within a title.

2.5.3.   Titles in quotation marks

Enclose in quotation marks, and do not underline, the titles of articles, essays, short stories, short poems, songs, chapters of books, unpublished works (such as lectures and speeches), and individual episodes of radio and television programs.

2.5.4.   Titles within titles

If a title indicated by quotation marks appears within an underlined title, retain the quotation marks. If a title indicated by underlining appears within a title enclosed by quotation marks, retain the underlining.

"Young Goodman Brown" and Hawthorne's Puritan Heritage

"As You Like It as a Pastoral Poem"

When a title normally indicated by quotation marks appears within another title requiring quotation marks, enclose the shorter title in single quotation marks.

"An Interpretation of Coleridge's 'Kubla Khan'"

When a normally underlined title appears within another underlined title, the incorporated title appears neither underlined nor in quotation marks.

Approaches to Teaching Camus's The Plague

2.5.5. Exceptions

The convention of using underlining or quotation marks to indicate titles does not apply to sacred writings (including all books and versions of the Bible); names of series, editions, and societies; descriptive words or phrases used instead of a title; and names of academic courses. None of these is underlined or put within quotation marks. (On capitalization, see 2.4.)

Sacred writings

Bible

King James Version

Old Testament

Genesis

Gospels

Talmud

Koran

Upanishads

Series

Bollingen Series

University of North Carolina Studies in Comparative Literature

Masterpiece Theatre

Editions

New Variorum Edition of Shakespeare

Centenary Edition of the Works of Nathaniel Hawthorne

Societies

```
American Medical Association

Renaissance Society of America
```

Descriptive words or phrases

```
Roosevelt's first inaugural address
```

Courses

```
Introduction to Calculus

Anthropology 102
```

The names of the divisions of a work are also not underlined or put within quotation marks. They are lowercased when used in the text or in documentation (except when following a period):

preface	chapter 2
introduction	act 4
bibliography	scene 7
appendix	stanza 20
index	canto 32

2.5.6.   Shortened titles

If you cite a title often in the text of your manuscript, you may, after stating the title in full at least once, use only a shortened title (preferably a familiar or an obvious one) or an abbreviation: "Nightingale" for "Ode to a Nightingale," *PL* for *Paradise Lost*. (For standard abbreviations of literary and religious works, see 6.6.)

2.6. Quotations

2.6.1. Accuracy of quotations

In general, a quotation — whether a word, phrase, sentence, or more — should correspond exactly to its source in spelling, capitalization, and interior punctuation. (On ellipses and other alterations of sources, see 2.6.4–5.)

2.6.2. Prose

Unless you wish to give special emphasis to prose quotations of not more than four typed lines, place them in quotation marks and incorporate them in the text.

"It was the best of times, it was the worst of times," writes

Charles Dickens of the eighteenth century.

"He was obeyed," writes Conrad of the company manager in Heart

of Darkness, "yet he inspired neither love nor fear, nor even

respect."

If you use a quotation of more than four typed lines — or if you wish to give a shorter quotation special emphasis — set it off from your text by beginning a new line, indenting ten spaces from the left margin, and typing it double-spaced, without adding quotation marks. A colon generally introduces a quotation displayed in this way, though sometimes the context may require a different mark of punctuation, or none at all. If you are quoting only a single paragraph, or part of one, do not indent the first line more than the rest.

At the conclusion of <u>Lord of the Flies</u> Ralph and the other
boys realize the horror of their actions:

> The tears began to flow and sobs shook him. He
> gave himself up to them now for the first time on
> the island; great, shuddering spasms of grief that
> seemed to wrench his whole body. His voice rose
> under the black smoke before the burning wreckage
> of the island; and infected by that emotion, the
> other little boys began to shake and sob too. And
> in the middle of them, with filthy body, matted
> hair, and unwiped nose, Ralph wept for the end of
> innocence. . . .

In quoting two or more paragraphs, indent the first line of each paragraph an additional three spaces. If, however, the first sentence quoted does not begin a paragraph in the source, do not indent it the additional three spaces. Indent only the first line of the following paragraph.

In <u>Moll Flanders</u>, Defoe maintains the pseudoautobiographical
narration typical of the picaresque tradition:

> My true name is so well known in the records or
> registers at Newgate, and in the Old Bailey, and
> there are some things of such consequence still
> depending there, relating to my particular conduct,
> that it is not to be expected I should set my name
> or the account of my family to this work. Perhaps,
> after my death, it may be better known; at present
> it would not be proper, no, not tho' a general

pardon should be issued, even without exceptions of

persons or crimes.

It is enough to tell you, that . . . some of my

worst comrades, who are out of the way of doing me

harm, having gone out of the world by the steps and

the string as I often expected to go, know me by the

name of Moll Flanders. . . .

2.6.3. Poetry

A quoted line of verse, or part of a line, should appear within quotation marks as part of your text, unless you wish to set it off for special emphasis. You may also incorporate two or three lines in this way, using a slash with a space on each side (/) to separate lines.

In Shakespeare's <u>Julius Caesar</u>, Antony says of Brutus, "This

was the noblest Roman of them all."

In <u>Julius Caesar</u>, Antony begins his famous speech: "Friends,

Romans, countrymen, lend me your ears; / I come to bury

Caesar, not to praise him."

A verse quotation of more than three lines should begin on a new line. Unless the quotation involves unusual spacing, indent each line ten spaces from the left margin and double-space between lines, adding no quotation marks that do not appear in the original. If the lines quoted are so long that a ten-space indentation would make the page look unbalanced, you may indent fewer than ten spaces from the margin. And if the spatial arrangement of the original, including indentation and spacing within and between lines, is unusual, reproduce it as accurately as possible.

E. E. Cummings concludes the poem with this vivid description of a carefree scene, reinforced by the carefree form of the lines themselves:

    it's

    spring

    and

        the

            goat-footed

    balloonMan   whistles

    far

    and

    wee

A quotation that begins in the middle of a line of verse should be reproduced in that way, not shifted to the left margin.

It is Jaques, in act 2 of <u>As You Like It</u>, who delivers the famous speech that compares the world to a stage:

            All the world's a stage

    And all the men and women merely players:

    They have their exits and their entrances;

    And one man in his time plays many parts,

        His acts being seven ages.

Jaques then proceeds to enumerate and analyze these ages.

If you quote lines of verse that are too long to reproduce line for line, indent each continuation five spaces more than the largest indentation and indicate at the right margin that this line is a "turnover" by typing "t/o" within square brackets.

```
           As if great Atlas from his Height

           Shou'd sink beneath his heavenly Weight,

     And, with a mighty Flaw, the flaming Wall

                 (As once it shall)

     Shou'd gape immense and rushing down, o'erwhelm

                 this neather Ball;        [t/o]

     So swift and so surprizing was our Fear:

     Our Atlas fell indeed; But Hercules was near.
```

See 5.4 for the placement of parenthetical references.

2.6.4. Ellipsis

When you wish to omit a word, phrase, sentence, or paragraph from a quoted passage, you should be guided by two principles: (1) fairness to the author quoted and (2) the grammatical integrity of your own writing. If you quote only a word or a phrase, it will be obvious that you have left out part of the original sentence.

```
In his inaugural address, John F. Kennedy spoke of a "new

frontier."
```

But if omitting material from the original leaves a quotation that appears to be a sentence, or a series of sentences, use ellipsis points, or spaced periods, to indicate that your quotation does not completely reproduce the original.

For ellipsis *within* a sentence, use three periods (. . .) with a space before and after each period.

Original

Medical thinking, trapped in the theory of astral influences, stressed air as the communicator of disease, ignoring sanitation or visible carriers. (Barbara W. Tuchman, *A Distant Mirror: The Calamitous Fourteenth Century*, 1978, New York: Ballantine, 1979, 101-02.)

Quoted with ellipsis in the middle

In seeking causes for plagues in the Middle Ages, as Barbara

W. Tuchman writes, "Medical thinking . . . stressed air as the

communicator of disease, ignoring sanitation or visible

carriers" (101-02).

When the ellipsis coincides with the end of your sentence, use three spaced periods following a sentence period — that is, four periods, with no space before the first.

Quoted with ellipsis at the end

In seeking causes for plagues in the Middle Ages, as Barbara

W. Tuchman writes, "Medical thinking, trapped in the theory of

astral influences, stressed air as the communicator of

disease. . . ."

If a parenthetical reference follows the ellipsis at the end of your sentence, use three spaced periods and place the sentence period after the final parenthesis.

Quoted with ellipsis at the end, followed by parenthetical reference

In seeking causes for plagues in the Middle Ages, as Barbara

W. Tuchman writes, "Medical thinking, trapped in the theory

of astral influences, stressed air as the communicator of

disease . . ." (101-02).

Four periods may also be used to indicate the omission of a whole sentence or more, or even of a paragraph or more. Remember, however, that grammatically complete sentences must both precede and follow the four periods.

Original

Presidential control reached its zenith under Andrew Jackson, the extent of whose attention to the press even before he became a candidate is suggested by the fact that he subscribed to twenty newspapers. Jackson was never content to have only one organ grinding out his tune. For a time, the *United States Telegraph* and the *Washington Globe* were almost equally favored as party organs, and there were fifty-seven journalists on the government payroll. (William L. Rivers, *The Mass Media: Reporting, Writing, Editing*, 2nd ed., New York: Harper, 1975, 7.)

Quoted with a sentence omitted

In discussing the historical relation between politics and the

press, William L. Rivers notes, "Presidential control reached

its zenith under Andrew Jackson. . . . For a time, the <u>United

States Telegraph</u> and the <u>Washington Globe</u> were almost equally

favored as party organs, and there were fifty-seven

journalists on the government payroll" (7).

2.6.5.   Other alterations of sources

Occasionally, you may decide that a quotation will be unclear or confusing to your reader unless you provide supplementary information.

While you may add material to a quoted source, just as you may omit
it, you should keep such contributions to a minimum and make sure to
distinguish them from the quotation, usually through a brief explanation in either parentheses or square brackets.

You may add an explanation in parentheses immediately after the closing quotation mark—for example, an indication that you have underlined
words for emphasis.

Lincoln specifically advocated a government "_for_ the people"

(emphasis added).

Such an indication may follow a reference in parentheses.

Houston Baker contends that "Trueblood's _duality_ is . . . also

that of his creator" (843; emphasis added).

Without the parenthetical addition, readers would assume that the words
underlined in these quotations are italicized in the originals. Sometimes
it may also be necessary to use "sic" ("thus," "so") in parentheses following a quotation to assure readers that the quotation is accurate even though
the spelling or logic might lead them to think otherwise.

The student referred to "Imitations of Immorality" (sic) as

one of Wordsworth's famous poems.

If your comment or explanation goes inside the quotation, then the
addition must appear within square brackets, not parentheses. (If your
typewriter does not include square brackets, insert them by hand.)

The title of the student's paper was "My Interpretation of

'Imitations of Immorality' [sic]."

Similarly, if a pronoun in a quotation seems unclear, you may follow it
immediately with an identification in square brackets.

```
Why, she would hang on him [Hamlet's

father]

As if increase of appetite had grown

By what it fed on. . . .
```

The accuracy of quotations in scholarly writing is extremely important. Extracts must reproduce the originals exactly. Unless you indicate deviations in brackets, take no liberties with the spelling or the punctuation of the source. In short, you must construct a clear, grammatically correct sentence that allows you to introduce or incorporate a quotation with complete accuracy. Alternatively, you can paraphrase the original and quote only fragments, which may be easier to integrate into the text. Methods vary, as the following example shows.

Original

Moralists have unanimously agreed, that unless virtue be nursed by liberty, it will never attain due strength — and what they say of man I extend to mankind, insisting that in all cases morals be fixed on immutable principles; and, that the being cannot be termed rational or virtuous, who obeys any authority, but that of reason. (Mary Wollstonecraft, *A Vindication of the Rights of Woman*, ed. Carol H. Poston, New York: Norton, 1975, 191.)

If you wish to begin your sentence with the sixth word of the Wollstonecraft passage ("unless"), you must capitalize the "u" and place it in brackets to indicate your alteration of the source. If you do not want to use square brackets, then recast your sentence to avoid the need for them.

```
Mary Wollstonecraft wrote that "unless virtue be nursed by

liberty, it will never attain due strength . . ." (191).
```

2.6.6. Punctuating quotations

The accurate quotation of sources, as we have seen, may involve parentheses for explanatory material outside a quotation, square brackets for interpolations within a quotation, and slashes between quoted lines of poetry incorporated into the text. In addition, a comma or a colon usually precedes a quotation. Use a colon before a quotation introduced formally, a comma or no punctuation before a quotation integrated into your sentence.

Shelley argued thus: "Poets are the unacknowledged legislators of the world."

but

Shelley thought poets "the unacknowledged legislators of the world."

or

"Poets," according to Shelley, "are the unacknowledged legislators of the world."

A colon normally introduces a quotation of verse, as it does a quotation set off from the text.

Coleridge's <u>Rime of the Ancient Mariner</u> concludes: "A sadder and a wiser man, / He rose the morrow morn."

Do not put quotation marks around quotations set off from the text, but generally reproduce internal punctuation exactly as it appears in the original. Use double quotation marks for quotations incorporated into the text, single quotation marks for quotations within those quotations.

The professor in the novel confessed that he found it "impossible to teach Hamlet's 'To be or not to be' speech" because he was terrified by its implications.

Although the internal punctuation of a quotation must remain intact, the closing punctuation depends on where the quoted material appears in your sentence. Suppose, for example, that you want to quote the following sentence.

You've got to be carefully taught.

If you begin your sentence with this line, you have to replace the closing period with a punctuation mark appropriate to the new context.

"You've got to be carefully taught," wrote Oscar Hammerstein

II of prejudice.

Commas and periods that directly follow quotations go *inside* the closing quotation marks, but a parenthetical reference should intervene between the quotation and the required punctuation. If a quotation ends with a single and a double quotation mark, the comma or period precedes both:

"Everyone can discern the cadences of 'Kubla Khan,'" the

instructor argued.

All other punctuation marks—such as semicolons, colons, question marks, and exclamation points—go outside quotation marks, except when they are part of the quoted material.

Original

I believe taxation without representation is tyranny!

Quoted

He attacked "taxation without representation" (32).

Did he attack "taxation without representation"?

He did not even attack "taxation without representation"!

but

He declared that "taxation without representation is tyranny!"

2.7.　Numbers

2.7.1.　Arabic numerals

Although there are still a few well-established uses for roman numerals (see 2.7.7), common practice today is to use arabic numerals to represent virtually all numbers. If your typewriter does not have the number "1," use a small letter el ("l"), not capital "I," for the arabic numeral.

2.7.2.　Use of words or numerals

In general, write as words all numbers from one to nine and use numerals for all numbers 10 and over (about 500 years ago, 17 pounds). But never begin a sentence with a numeral (Five hundred years ago. . . .). Always use numerals with abbreviations and symbols (6 lbs., 8KB, 4 p.m., $9, 3%, 2′) and in addresses (5 13th Ave.), dates (1 April 1984), decimal fractions (8.3), and page references (page 7). For very large numbers you may use a combination of numerals and words: 4.5 million. Related numbers must be expressed in the same style: 5 of the 217 casualties, 3 automobiles and 12 trucks, from 1 billion to 1.2 billion.

In discussions that require few numbers, you may spell out those that can be written in no more than two words and represent other numbers by numerals (one, thirty-six, ninety-nine, one hundred, fifteen hundred, two thousand, three million; *but* 2½, 101, 137, and 1,275).

2.7.3.　Commas in numbers

Commas are usually placed between the third and fourth digits from the right, the sixth and seventh, and so on.

```
1,000    20,000    7,654,321
```

Exceptions to this practice include page and line numbers, street numbers, and four-digit year numbers. Commas are added in longer year numbers.

On page 3322. . . .

At 4132 Broadway. . . .

In 1984. . . .

but

In 20,000 BC. . . .

2.7.4. Percentages and amounts of money

Treat percentages and amounts of money as you do other numbers: use numerals with the appropriate symbols (1%, 45%, 100%, $5.35, $35, $2,000, 68¢). In discussions with few numbers, you may spell out percentages and amounts of money if you can do so in no more than two words (five dollars, forty-five percent, two thousand dollars, sixty-eight cents). Do not combine spelled forms of numbers with symbols.

2.7.5. Dates

Be consistent in writing dates: use either "22 July 1986" or "July 22, 1986," but not both. (If you begin with the month, add a comma after the day and also after the year, unless another punctuation mark goes there, such as a period or a question mark.) Do not use a comma between the month and the year: August 1984.

Spell out centuries in lowercase letters (the twentieth century) and hyphenate them as adjectives (eighteenth-century thought, nineteenth- and twentieth-century literature). Decades are usually written out without capitalization (the eighties), but it is becoming acceptable to express them in figures: the 1980s or the '80s.

"BC" follows the year, but "AD" precedes it: 19 BC, AD 565. Some writers use "BCE" 'before the Common Era' and "CE" 'Common Era' (37 BCE, CE 467). European usage gives all dates in day-month-year order, separated by spaces, commas, hyphens, periods, or slash marks. To indicate both Western and non-Western dates, put one set in parentheses: 3 November 1693 (K'ang hsi 32/10/6).

2.7.6. Inclusive numbers

In indicating a range of numbers, give the second number in full for numbers through 99: 2-3, 10-12, 21-48, 89-99. For larger numbers, give only the last two digits of the second number, unless more are necessary: 96-101, 103-04, 395-401, 923-1003, 1003-05, 1608-774. In giving a range of years, write both in full unless they are within the same century: 1898-1901, 1898-99.

2.7.7. Roman numerals

Use capital roman numerals for primary divisions of an outline and for individuals in a series: Henry VIII, John Paul II, Elizabeth II. Use lowercase roman numerals for citing pages of a book that are so numbered (e.g., the pages in a preface). Some scholars prefer to use roman numerals to designate acts and scenes of plays: "In *Othello* IV.ii we begin to see that. . . ."

2.8. Transliteration and romanization

In most general studies, quotations and citations from alphabets other than the Latin alphabet should be transliterated and the spoken forms of nonalphabetic languages should be transcribed in the Latin alphabet (romanized). In studies with extensive quotations from Greek, however, the Greek alphabet is usually used.

Listed below are the systems of transliteration or romanization recommended for most general scholarly studies. In linguistic studies, non-Latin alphabets are normally reproduced (often by hand), and publishers may ask authors to provide carefully written copies of the non-Latin characters to be reproduced. The systems below that are cited from *Cataloging Service*, the bulletin of the Library of Congress Processing Department, have been approved by the American Library Association and the Library of Congress. The complete set of *Cataloging Service* has been reprinted in two volumes by Gale Research Co. (1980).

Amharic: *Cataloging Service* 104 (1972): 14-16; rpt. 118 (1976): 13-14.
Arabic: *American National Standard System for the Romanization of Arabic.* New York: Amer. Natl. Standards Inst., 1972. Z39.12-1972.

Armenian: *American National Standard System for the Romanization of Armenian.* New York: Amer. Natl. Standards Inst., 1979. Z39.37–1979.

Assamese: *Cataloging Service* 64 (1964): 2; rpt. 118 (1976): 23.

Belorussian: *Cataloging Service* 118 (1976): 25. Corrected in 119 (1976): 18; 122 (1977): 11. See also J. Thomas Shaw, *The Transliteration of Modern Russian for English-Language Publications* (1967, New York: MLA, 1979), and *American National Standard System for the Romanization of Slavic Cyrillic Characters* (New York: Amer. Natl. Standards Inst., 1976, Z39.24–1976).

Bengali: *Cataloging Service* 64 (1964): 3; rpt. 118 (1976): 27.

Bulgarian: Select the appropriate system from those given for Russian in J. Thomas Shaw, *The Transliteration of Modern Russian for English-Language Publications* (1967, New York: MLA, 1979), and transliterate from the corresponding Russian form. See also *American National Standard System for the Romanization of Slavic Cyrillic Characters* (New York: Amer. Natl. Standards Inst., 1976, Z39.24–1976).

Burmese: *Cataloging Service* 76 (1966): 2–5; rpt. 118 (1976): 31–34.

Chinese: Use the pinyin system of transcription. See *Reform of the Chinese Written Language* (Peking: Foreign Languages, 1958).

Church Slavonic: Select the appropriate system from those given for Russian in J. Thomas Shaw, *The Transliteration of Modern Russian for English-Language Publications* (1967, New York: MLA, 1979), and transliterate from the corresponding Russian form. See also *American National Standard System for the Romanization of Slavic Cyrillic Characters* (New York: Amer. Natl. Standards Inst., 1976, Z39.24–1976).

Georgian: *Cataloging Service* 119 (1976): 29. Corrected in 120 (1977): 9.

Greek: *Cataloging Service* 104 (1972): 17–18; rpt. 118 (1976): 59.

Gujarti: *Cataloging Service* 64 (1964): 4; rpt. 118 (1976): 61.

Hebrew: Select the appropriate system from those given in *American National Standard Romanization of Hebrew* (New York: Amer. Natl. Standards Inst., 1975, Z39.25–1975).

Hindi: *Cataloging Service* 64 (1964): 5–6; rpt. 119 (1976): 31–32.

Japanese: *American National Standard System for the Romanization of Japanese.* New York: Amer. Natl. Standards Inst., 1972. Z39.11–1972. See *Cataloging Service* 119 (1976): 33–41 for guidelines on word division.

Kannada: *Cataloging Service* 64 (1964): 7; rpt. 119 (1976): 43.

Kashmiri: *Cataloging Service* 31 (1954): 2.

Khmer: *American National Standard System for the Romanization of Lao, Khmer, and Pali.* New York: Amer. Natl. Standards Inst., 1979. Z39.35–1979.

Korean: The McCune-Reischauer system, as described in "The Romanization of the Korean Language" (*Transactions of the Korean Branch, Royal Asiatic Society* 29 [1939]: 1–55).

Lao: *American National Standard System for the Romanization of Lao, Khmer, and Pali*. New York: Amer. Natl. Standards Inst., 1979. Z39.35–1979.

Macedonian: *Cataloging Service* 120 (1977): 37.

Malayalam: *Cataloging Service* 64 (1964): 8; rpt. 119 (1976): 47.

Marathi: *Cataloging Service* 64 (1964): 9; rpt. 119 (1976): 51.

Non-Slavic languages in the Cyrillic alphabet: *Cataloging Service* 122 (1977): 27; 123 (1977): 15; 124 (1978): 31–34; 125 (1978): 25–27.

Oriya: *Cataloging Service* 64 (1964): 10; rpt. 119 (1976): 53.

Pali: *American National Standard System for the Romanization of Lao, Khmer, and Pali*. New York: Amer. Natl. Standards Inst., 1979. Z39.35–1979.

Panjabi: *Cataloging Service* 64 (1964): 11; rpt. 119 (1976): 55.

Persian: *Cataloging Service* 92 (1970): 1–5; rpt. 119 (1976): 57–61.

Prakrit: *Cataloging Service* 64 (1964): 12; rpt. 120 (1977): 35.

Pushto: *Cataloging Service* 93 (1970): 1–5; rpt. 120 (1977): 29–31.

Russian: Shaw, J. Thomas. *The Transliteration of Modern Russian for English-Language Publications*. 1967. New York: MLA, 1979.

Sanskrit: *Cataloging Service* 64 (1964): 12; rpt. 120 (1977): 35.

Serbian: *Cataloging Service* 120 (1977): 37.

Sindhi: *Cataloging Service* 104 (1972): 19–20; rpt. 120 (1977): 39–40.

Sinhalese: *Cataloging Service* 88 (1970): 11; rpt. 120 (1977): 41.

Tamil: *Cataloging Service* 64 (1964): 13; rpt. 120 (1977): 43.

Telugu: *Cataloging Service* 64 (1964): 14; rpt. 120 (1977): 45.

Thai: *American National Standard System for the Romanization of Lao, Khmer, and Pali*. New York: Amer. Natl. Standards Inst., 1979. Z39.35–1979.

Tibetan: *Cataloging Service* 90 (1970): 4; rpt. 120 (1977): 49.

Ukrainian: *American National Standard System for the Romanization of Slavic Cyrillic Characters*. New York: Amer. Natl. Standards Inst., 1976. Z39.24–1976.

Urdu: *Cataloging Service* 94 (1970): 1–7; rpt. 120 (1977): 53–58.

Yiddish: *Cataloging Service* 118 (1976): 63.

3 PREPARING THE SCHOLARLY MANUSCRIPT

3.1. Physical characteristics

3.1.1. Typing

Use fresh black ribbon and clean type. Avoid typewriters with "script" or other fancy print; do not use "script" to indicate italics. Type on only one side of the paper; do not use the other side for any purpose. Be sure to keep a copy of each manuscript submitted.

3.1.2. Paper

Use white, 20-pound, 8½- by 11-inch paper. If you cannot obtain 8½- by 11-inch paper, use the closest size available. In no case, however, type in an area larger than 6½ by 9 inches. Do not submit a manuscript typed on erasable paper, which smudges easily. If you find erasable paper convenient to use, submit a photocopy on "plain" (not coated) paper. Never use thin paper except for a carbon copy.

3.1.3. Margins

Except for page numbers, leave one-inch margins at the top and bottom and on both sides of the text. (For placement of page numbers, see 3.1.5.) Indent the first word of a paragraph five spaces from the left margin. Indent a setoff quotation ten spaces from the left margin. (For examples and exceptions, see 2.6.2–3.)

3.1.4. Spacing

Double-space the entire typescript, including the title, quotations, notes, and bibliography.

3.1.5. Page numbers

Paginate consecutively throughout the manuscript, numbering *every* page in the upper right-hand corner, one-half inch from the top. (See 3.2 for the form of the first page of the manuscript.) From page 2 on, type an abbreviated title of your work before each page number. (You may type your last name instead if anonymity is not required.) Do not punctuate a page number by adding a period, a hyphen, or any other mark or symbol (such as the abbreviation "p.").

Although in writing the chapters of a book or separate essays for a collection, authors may paginate each chapter or essay separately, the manuscript submitted for publication should be numbered consecutively from beginning to end. In a work with several authors, the name preceding each page number should be that of the author who is to receive the copyedited manuscript and proof of that page.

3.1.6. Corrections and revisions

Proofread and correct the typescript carefully before offering it to a publisher, but remember that typescripts submitted for consideration should be as neat as possible. Likewise, if an editor or publisher has accepted your manuscript but has requested revisions before copyediting, make all revisions clear, legible, and unambiguous, to avoid problems during typesetting.

You may type brief corrections and revisions (or write them neatly and legibly in ink) directly above the lines involved, using carets ($\wedge$) to indicate where they go. Do not write below a line or use the margins. Marginal corrections accompanied by proofreading symbols are appropriate only for works set in type (or stored on some medium other than typescript).

Retype any page that requires numerous or substantial changes. If the resulting page is shorter than the original, leave it so, drawing a line from the last line of text to the bottom of the page to indicate that the text on the next page follows immediately (without intervening space). If the revised version will not fit on one page, continue it on a separate page, repeating the page number, adding the letter *A* (e.g., "32A," to follow page 32), and drawing a line from the last line of text to the bottom of the page if the new page is shorter than normal. Indicate at the bottom of the page that a specially numbered page follows (e.g., "page 32A follows"). If there are many specially numbered pages, renumber the pages of the entire typescript consecutively before submitting it.

Although you may type an insertion on a separate page (labeled, e.g., "insert to page 32") and clearly mark the typescript to show where it goes, the cut-and-paste method is preferable: cut the original typescript at the place of the insert, tape the top portion of the page to a new sheet, type the insert in place, and then tape the balance of the original page to the new sheet, carrying over any excess to a specially numbered page. If you follow this procedure, do not submit the "original" typewritten copy with its taped insertion but provide a clear photocopy, to avoid the possibility of losing the taped portions of the typescript.

Whatever system you adopt should result in a neat, legible typescript in proper order.

3.1.7. Binding

Secure essay-length manuscripts by paper clips — never staples. Use a rubber band around book-length manuscripts and do not secure individual chapters in any way.

3.2. Titles of manuscripts

3.2.1. Placement

If you are preparing a manuscript for a particular journal or publisher, follow the publisher's instructions or, in the absence of specific instructions, the appropriate instructions below. If you plan to submit a manuscript seriatim to journals or publishers until it is accepted, prepare it in accordance with the instructions below for anonymous submission.

A manuscript for a journal with a policy of anonymous submissions should include a separate, unnumbered page giving the title and your name, address, and telephone number (along with any temporary addresses you foresee over the next two years). Number the first page of the manuscript proper and repeat the title one inch from the top of the page, flush left. Then double-space twice and begin the essay, thus leaving space for your name to be added following acceptance.

A manuscript for a journal that does not require anonymity does not need a separate title page. Instead, number the first page in the upper right-hand corner (one-half inch from the top), double-space twice, and then type your name, address, telephone number, and any temporary addresses flush with the left margin, double-spacing between lines. Double-space twice to the title (flush left), and double-space between the lines of the title if it has more than one. Double-space again and type your name (flush left) exactly as you wish it to appear in the journal. Double-space between your name and the first line of the text.

A manuscript for a book should bear a separate title page with the same information given for a journal requiring anonymous submission. Individual chapters should not have separate title pages, but each should begin on a new page. Type "Chapter" and the chapter number flush left one inch from the top, double-space, and then type the chapter title flush left.

If you are contributing a chapter or an essay to a collection by several authors, type your name, address, telephone number, and any temporary addresses on the first page, beginning flush left one inch from the top and double-spacing throughout. Then double-space to the title, double-space and repeat your name, and double-space to the first line of the text. For the title-page format of a dissertation, see 7.5.

3.2.2.   Capitalization and punctuation

Do not underline your title or put it in quotation marks or type it in all capital letters. Follow the rules for capitalization in 2.4.1, and underline only those words that you would underline in the text (see 2.2.8).

```
The Attitude toward Violence in Anthony Burgess's A Clockwork

Orange

Vergil and the Locus Amoenus Tradition in Latin Literature

The Use of the Noun Chevisaunce in Chaucer and Spenser
```

Do not use a period after your title or after any heading, including numerals used alone as section heads (see 3.3.3). A title ordinarily does not carry a symbol or number referring to a note, though an editor will occasionally add a note to the title to cite the source of the work.

3.3.   Divisions of the text

3.3.1.   General

Although scholarly articles published in the humanities often have no formal divisions, related groups of paragraphs may be separated from the preceding and following groups of paragraphs by extra space (four lines in a typescript). When such a break appears between pages of a typescript, type "[extra space]" on the first line of the next page, using square brackets as shown, double-space, and proceed with the text.

If you give unified sections of thought numbers or numbers and headings, type these designations flush left, with no extra spacing above or below. Use arabic numerals, and separate a heading from a preceding number by a period and a space.

2. From 1965 to 1984

Long articles frequently have formal divisions, and books often have even more complex systems of subordination. The principles governing the formal divisions of a long paper are the same as those for the sections of a chapter (see 3.3.2-3).

The major divisions of a book usually appear in the following order (although only the words not given in brackets will serve as titles, you can aid your editor by typing each of the others, in square brackets as shown, flush left one inch from the top of the appropriate pages):

[title page]
[verso of title page, or copyright page]
[dedication] (optional)
[epigraph] (optional)
Contents (the table of contents)
Illustrations (if applicable; a list of illustrations)
Tables (if applicable; a list of tables)
Foreword (optional)
Preface (optional)
Acknowledgments (often combined with the preface)
Introduction (optional)
[text]
Appendix (optional)
Notes (optional)

Glossary (optional)
Works Cited (the list of works cited)
Index (optional)

The most common divisions of a book, within the text itself, are chapters (see 3.3.3). Chapters should be numbered consecutively throughout a book, whether or not they are grouped into "parts," and should usually be given titles. Parts comprising related chapters should also be numbered consecutively and may be given titles.

3.3.2.   Consistency of heads

Part titles, chapter titles, and titles of divisions within a chapter are generally referred to as "heads." Insofar as possible, make parallel heads parallel in grammatical form. Sometimes, however, as in this manual, clarity and common usage require violation of this principle. Yet even then, the heads should be as grammatically similar as possible (e.g., avoid shifting from sentences to single words for parallel heads within a chapter).

If you adopt number and letter designations for heads, be absolutely consistent, and use no "1" unless there is a "2," no "a" unless there is a "b." (The only exception to this last principle may occur in highly schematized works where the absence of a particular number or letter in a section indicates that there is no material to include under that designation. It is often clearer to the reader merely to list the head and then go on to the next head. Common sense and the number of heads not followed by text will dictate the appropriate choice.)

3.3.3.   Levels of heads

You can save your editor a lot of trouble and perhaps your publisher considerable expense by carefully distinguishing the levels of heads in your manuscript. Listing all heads in outline form is the simplest way to establish the coordination and subordination of heads, particularly in a long manuscript (and you should give your publisher a copy of this outline).

In book manuscripts, part numbers and titles are normally centered on separate sheets of paper. Type "part title" in square brackets one inch from the top of the page.

Indicating the proper coordination and subordination of heads within a manuscript (once they have been established) is not always easy. Ordinarily, do not attempt to distinguish levels of heads typographically, because the few variations possible on a typewriter — for example, all-capital heads and underlined heads — may cause problems for the editor and typesetter. It is usually far better to indicate levels of heads with letters in square brackets. Type these designations flush left, and then type the heads, beginning each with a capital and continuing with lowercase letters.

One convention is to designate chapter titles "A" heads, the next lower level "B" heads, and so on. Under this system, the heads of this chapter would have been typed as follows:

```
Chapter 3

[A] Preparing the scholarly manuscript

[B] Physical characteristics

[C] Typing

[C] Paper

. . . . . . . . . . . . .

[B] Titles of manuscripts
```

Another system is to number heads, as in this manual. Place such numbers in square brackets to indicate that they should not be printed (they would normally be printed only in certain linguistic studies and in reference works). Under this system, the heads of this chapter would have been typed as follows:

```
Chapter 3

Preparing the scholarly manuscript

[3.1] Physical characteristics

[3.1.1] Typing

[3.1.2] Paper
```

Whatever system you adopt should make immediately clear to the editor, copy editor, designer, and typesetter the proper coordination and subordination of heads. The publisher will decide on the typographical specifications for each level of head you designate. The keys you provide will not, of course, appear in type, but they will ensure the appropriate placement, capitalization, and typeface of the various heads. Using such a system will avoid confusion, costly changes in display type (which is often seen by an author only in page proof, if at all), and needless queries about the use of uppercase and accents.

3.4. Tables and illustrations

Place illustrative material as close as possible to the part of the text that it illustrates. A table is usually labeled "Table," given an arabic numeral, and captioned. Type both label and caption flush left on separate lines above the table and capitalize them as you would a title (do not use all capital letters; see 2.4.1). Give the source of the table and any notes immediately below the table. To avoid confusion between notes to the text and notes to the table, use lowercase letters rather than numerals for notes to the table. Double-space throughout, providing ruled lines as needed. (See example on facing page.)

Any other type of illustrative material—for example, a photograph, map, line drawing, graph, or chart—should be labeled "Fig." (for "Figure"), assigned an arabic numeral, and given a title or caption: Fig. 1. Albrecht Dürer, *Self-Portrait*, Prado, Madrid. A label, title, or caption should include the source of the illustrative material and a statement of permission to reproduce it (if needed; see 1.9.2) and ordinarily appears directly below the illustration, flush with the left margin.

3.5. Preparing manuscripts in machine-readable form

3.5.1. General

The "manuscript" of a work composed on a word-processing system resides in a computer disk or tape, and the printed-out (paper) version is no longer itself the original but, rather, merely one step in the development of the article or book. More and more scholars, like other authors, are using such systems, and the next edition of this manual will probably be written with the assumption that all scholarly manuscripts are produced

Table 1

Institutions of Higher Education in the United States

Type of institution	Public	Private	Total
Doctoral-granting universities	108	65	173
Comprehensive colleges and			
universities	308	145	453
Liberal arts colleges	28	691	719
Two-year institutions	805	256	1,061
Specialized institutions[a]	64	357	421
Total	1,313	1,514	2,827

Source: ADE Bulletin 45 (1975): 1.

[a] This group consists mainly of seminaries and medical, engineering, and law schools.

in machine-readable form for automatic typesetting. But in this transitional stage of the application of word-processing procedures to scholarly publication it is essential to distinguish between two uses of this technology and the conventions to be followed for each.

3.5.2.   Manuscripts for traditional publication

Scholars preparing manuscripts on a word-processing system for traditional publication can easily make insertions and deletions and present final typescripts without any noticeable corrections. Usually, however, these typescripts will be edited in the traditional way and then set in type. As of this writing, most publishers have not devised practical procedures for working directly with an author's stored version of the manuscript.

When a publisher asks for revisions *before accepting* a typescript, the author may work on a word-processing system and submit a clean copy for consideration. Once a typescript has been accepted, however, most editors will insist that it not be retyped, since they need a clear record of all the changes suggested, whether made or rejected, in preparing a work for publication. After final acceptance typescripts produced on a word processor should be treated like traditional manuscripts, unless the publisher has agreed to some other procedure beforehand.

Working on a word processor sometimes creates problems, however, because the traditional designations used in scholarly manuscripts are not available on some word-processing systems, which may offer features more appropriate to business purposes than to scholarly ones. For example, a scholarly manuscript should never be "justified" at the right margin, since the spaces required for this justification are at best a hindrance to editors and publishers and often a source of unnecessary confusion. Whenever it is not practical to follow standard conventions on a word processor, adopt reasonable alternatives and use them consistently. Include a list of these alternatives when you submit the manuscript for consideration. Insofar as possible, adopting reasonable alternatives is preferable to inserting characters by hand on a typescript produced by a word-processing system. The alternatives suggested here deal with the most common problems; whatever system you devise, do not rely on characters and symbols (particularly parentheses) commonly used with conventional meanings in scholarly writing.

a. Lack of superscripts. Some word-processing systems cannot produce the superscripts traditionally used for note numbers. Numbers enclosed in slashes are an acceptable alternative.

traditional	acceptable alternative	not acceptable
the sentence.[1]	the sentence./1/	the sentence.(1)

b. Lack of diacritical marks. For some scholars the lack of diacritical marks is the most troublesome deficiency that a word-processing system can have, since inserting such marks by hand throughout various versions of a typescript is so tedious and prone to error that it nearly offsets the advantages of the technology. A better method is to represent diacritical marks on your word processor in a consistent manner that graphically resembles the accents as nearly as possible.

traditional	acceptable alternatives	not acceptable
ä	a/"/	a("), a"
á	a/'/	a('), a'
à	a/`/, a/!/	a(`), a`, a(!), a!
ç	c/,/	c(,), c,

3.5.3.   Manuscripts for automatic typesetting

Within a few years, most scholarly journals and books will probably be typeset directly from floppy disks or other machine-readable media supplied by their authors. Currently, however, machinery and software are generally insufficiently compatible to allow for efficient use of automatic typesetting. If you have access to word-processing equipment, ask your publisher for guidelines on the preparation of your manuscript for automatic typesetting. If you do not yet have a publisher, you will have to adopt generic coding in preparing machine-readable disks.

In either case, you should follow certain general principles. Do not justify right margins and do not hyphenate words at the ends of lines (doing either on some word-processing systems would introduce characters and fixed spaces that would only have to be removed later). Only those spaces and hyphens that are to appear in print should be used — for example, the spaces between words and the hyphens in certain compound terms. Type all copy flush left, with no exceptions (even for lists, bibliographies, and quotations set off from the text). Neither center nor indent any material, even the openings of paragraphs. Mark the end of a paragraph by two carriage returns; otherwise use the carriage return only at the ends of items in a list (or at any time the next material must begin a new line, as at the ends of lines of poetry).

Quotation marks should be indicated thus:

```
opening single quotes  ''

opening double quotes  ""

closing single quotes  '

closing double quotes  "
```

Consequently, the quotation marks for a translation directly following a foreign term would appear *ainsi* ''thus'; those for a title would appear as '' ''The Process of Discovery.''

Use each key for only one meaning: the letter *l* cannot serve as the numeral one; letter *O* cannot be used as a zero; any special characters must be used with only one meaning. In a manuscript that occasionally requires so many different characters from another alphabet that you cannot assign each its own key, you could select one character to represent them all; in this cumbersome procedure you have to mark the correct character for each occurrence and the publisher has to insert appropriate typesetting commands manually. If your work involves frequent use of special characters, ask your publisher to supply special codes or devise them yourself as suggested below in the discussion of second keyboards.

If your publisher cannot supply codes for you to use on your word-processing system or if you have not yet chosen a publisher, you may use generic codes to indicate both the type of material that follows (e.g., a chapter title, an A-level head, or text) and the typeface (e.g., roman, italic, or bold). Codes should be used to indicate only the required uses of the various typefaces, not to design the final appearance of the book or article. In devising generic codes, first select a character, called a delimiter, to distinguish codes from copy to be printed. The delimiter is typed before and after each code and cannot be used with any other function in your manuscript. The best delimiters are characters available on the word processor but not used in scholarly writing (such as < >, { }, @), invalid combinations of characters (such as $ followed by letters), or invalid combinations of punctuation (such as ,; ;,). The following sample generic codes are taken from *An Author's Primer to Word Processing* (©1983 by the Association of American Publishers and used with permission); they are shown here with braces as the delimiter:

{pn}   part number

{pt}   part title

{pst}   part subtitle

{cn}   chapter number

{ct}   chapter title

{cst}   chapter subtitle

{h1}   first-level head

{h2}   second-level head

{h3}	third-level head, etc.
{tx}	text
{nl}	numbered list
{unl}	unnumbered list
{li}	list item
{ext}	extract
{fn}	footnote (i.e., the note itself)
{fnref}	footnote reference (i.e., the note number in the text and in the note itself)
{fgn}	figure number
{fgt}	figure title
{sn}	source note (used for tables and figures)
{tn}	table number
{tt}	table title
{tch}	table column head
{tb}	table body
{tfn}	table footnote
{gl}	glossary
{ref}	reference (i.e., a listing in a list of works cited)
{r}	roman typeface
{i}	italic typeface
{b}	bold typeface

You may construct additional generic codes if necessary, though those listed should suffice in all but exceptional cases. Each code applies until you cancel it by typing a conflicting code: for example, once you type {tx}, everything that follows will be text until you type a countermand, such as {fnref}; similarly, once you type {r}, everything that follows will be in roman typeface until you type another typeface code, {i} or {b}.

If your manuscript requires many special characters, such as Greek letters or phonetic symbols, you may choose to construct a "second keyboard," assigning new values to all the standard keys on the keyboard. You can indicate a second keyboard, often called an "escape keyboard," by the code {2} or, for Greek letters, by {g}. When you submit your manuscript to the publisher, include a list of all the keys used on this second keyboard; if you already have a publisher, consult the publisher for how to handle such special characters.

Unless your publisher instructs you otherwise, accompany the machine-readable version of your manuscript with a printed-out (paper) version.

3.5.4.   Manuscripts for optical character recognition

Optical-character-recognition (OCR) machines can recognize, optically, either special OCR characters or characters typed on a conventional typewriter or word processor, and they can create a magnetic tape, for typesetting, by "reading" a manuscript. If your publisher asks you to prepare your manuscript for optical character recognition, obtain from the publisher any special instructions; otherwise, follow the suggestions in 3.5.2 or 3.5.3.

For optical character recognition, a clean, dark ribbon copy is essential; dot-matrix printers, unless of the highest quality, are not acceptable.

OCR can also be applied in resetting a work, as in preparing a new edition; the machine optically scans the copy text to produce a new typesetting, which the editor then corrects. To be useful, such a procedure requires close cooperation between author and publisher.

3.5.5.   Further information

Common generic coding for the automatic typesetting of manuscripts may be forthcoming within the next few years. With the support of the Council on Library Resources, the Association of American Publishers is sponsoring a project to develop such coding.

For additional information about the use of word processing and other forms of technology in scholarly writing, consult the following works:

An Author's Primer to Word Processing. New York: Assn. of Amer. Publishers, 1983.

McKenzie, Alan T., ed. *A Grin on the Interface: Word Processing for the Academic Humanist.* Technology and the Humanities 1. New York: MLA, 1984.

4 PREPARING THE LIST OF WORKS CITED

4.1. General guidelines

In scholarly writing, all borrowed material—whether facts, opinions, or quotations—must be documented. This manual recommends acknowledging sources by keying citations in the text to a list of the research materials used. Although this list appears at the end of the manuscript, you must draft it in advance so that you can refer to it parenthetically throughout the text. This chapter explains how to prepare the list of works cited; the next chapter demonstrates how to document sources in the text. (For information concerning other systems of documentation, such as endnotes and footnotes, see 5.7–8.)

The **Works Cited** section lists all works that have contributed ideas and information to your manuscript. The list simplifies documentation because it permits you to make only brief references to these works in the text. A citation such as "(Thompson 32–35)" enables readers to identify the source in the list of works cited. The title "Works Cited" is usually preferable to the other names for such a list, **Bibliography** (literally, "description of books") and **Literature Cited**, since it allows the inclusion of not only books and articles but also nonprint sources.

Titles used for other kinds of source lists include **Annotated Bibliography**, **Works Consulted**, and **Selected Bibliography**. An annotated bibliography, or an **Annotated List of Works Cited**, contains descriptive or evaluative comments on the sources.

Thompson, Stith. The Folktale. New York: Dryden, 1946. A

comprehensive survey of the most popular folktales,

including their histories and their uses in literary

works.

The title "Works Consulted" indicates that the list is not confined to works cited in the paper. A selected bibliography, or a **Selected List of Works Consulted**, suggests readings in the field.

A bibliographic description includes detailed technical information about a book. For example, in Fredson Bowers's edition of Stephen Crane's

The Red Badge of Courage (Charlottesville: UP of Virginia, 1975, 244–45), the bibliographic description of the novel begins as follows:

> The Red Badge / Of Courage / [red: plumed helmet orn.] / An Episode of the American Civil War / [red: 5 plume orn.] / By / [red: 4 plume orn.] / Stephen Crane / [red: 3 plume orn.] / [Appleton device] / [red: 2 plume orn.] / [red: 3 plume orn.] / New York / D. Appleton and Company / 1895

Bowers continues with information on, among other things, the collation, the contents ("pp. i–ii: blank; p. iii: title-page . . . "), the binding ("Light yellow brown . . . "), and the dust jacket. For a thorough analysis of the problems involved in bibliographic description, see Bowers, *Principles of Bibliographical Description* (1949; New York: Russell, 1962).

4.2.   Placement

The list of works cited appears at the end of the scholarly work; in a book or dissertation it precedes only the index. Occasionally, as in textbooks or collections of pieces by different authors, each chapter or essay ends with its own list.

Start the list of works cited on a new page. Number each page of the list, continuing the sequence of the text, in the upper right-hand corner, one-half inch from the top. Center the title "Works Cited" one inch from the top of the page. Double-space between the title and the first entry. Begin the entry flush with the left margin. If an entry runs more than one line, indent the subsequent line or lines five spaces from the left margin. Double-space the entire list, between entries as well as within entries. Continue the list on as many pages as necessary.

4.3.   Arrangement

In general, alphabetize entries in the list of works cited by the author's last name or, if the author's name is unknown, by the first word in the title other than a definite or an indefinite article (*An Encyclopedia of the Latin-American Novel* would be alphabetized under *e*; *Le théâtre en France au Moyen Age* under *t*). The alphabetical listing, as we explain at greater length in the next chapter, makes it easy for the reader to find full publication information for works referred to in the text.

Other kinds of bibliographies may be arranged differently. An annotated list, a list of works consulted, or a list of selected readings for a historical study, for example, may be organized chronologically by publication date. Some bibliographies are divided into sections, with the items alphabetized in each. A list may be broken down into primary sources and secondary sources or into different research media: books, articles, and recordings. Alternatively, it may be arranged by subject matter (e.g., Literature and Law, Law in Literature, Law as Literature), by period (e.g., Classical Utopia, Renaissance Utopia), or by area (e.g., Egyptian Mythology, Greek Mythology, Norse Mythology).

4.4.   Citing books: Information required

4.4.1.   General guidelines

An entry in a list of works cited characteristically has three main divisions — author, title, and publication information — each followed by a period and two spaces.

Frye, Northrop. Anatomy of Criticism: Four Essays.

   Princeton: Princeton UP, 1957.

Sometimes, however, other facts are required, and a period and two spaces follow each additional item of information.

Porter, Katherine Anne. "Pale Horse, Pale Rider." Norton

   Anthology of World Masterpieces. Ed. Maynard Mack et al.

   4th ed. 2 vols. New York: Norton, 1979. 2: 1606-47.

In citing books, normally arrange the information in the following order:

1. Author's name
2. Title of the part of the book
3. Title of the book
4. Name of the editor, translator, or compiler
5. Edition used
6. Number of volumes

7. Name of the series
8. Place of publication, name of the publisher, and date of publication
9. Page numbers
10. Supplementary bibliographic information and annotation

Each of these items of information is discussed in general terms in 4.4.2–11; examples of these recommendations are given in 4.5.

4.4.2.   Author's name

Reverse the author's name for alphabetizing, adding a comma after the last name: Porter, Katherine Anne. Follow the name with a period and leave two spaces before beginning the next item.

Always give the author's name as it appears on the title page. Never abbreviate a name given in full. If, for example, the title page lists the author as "Carleton Brown" do not enter the book under "Brown, C." Conversely, if the title page shows an initial for a name (T. S. Eliot), do not spell out the name in full. You may use square brackets, however, to indicate a full name not found in the work cited if you think this additional information would be helpful to readers. You might supply it, for example, if you use the full name in your text or if another source uses it.

Lewis, C[live] S[taples].

Nesbit, E[dith].

Tolkien, J[ohn] R[onald] R[euel].

Similarly, use square brackets if you wish to indicate the real name of an author listed under a pseudonym.

Eliot, George [Mary Ann Evans].

Novalis [Friedrich von Hardenberg].

If the name of the author is known but not stated on the title page, give the name in brackets; add a question mark if the authorship is not universally accepted.

[Medici, Lorenzo de' ?]. <u>Nencia da Barberino</u>.

Occasionally, it is more appropriate to begin an entry by naming not the author but the editor or translator (see 4.5.2, 4.5.12–13). To cite an anonymous book or a book by a corporate author, see 4.5.6–7; a work written by more than one author, 4.5.4; two or more books by the same author or authors, 4.5.3–4.

4.4.3. Title of the part of a book

In general, follow the recommendations for titles given in 2.5. To cite only a part of a book, state the title or name of the part of the book after the author's name. To cite a work in an anthology (e.g., an essay, a short story, a poem, or a play), see 4.5.8; a book division that has only a general name, such as an introduction or a preface, 4.5.9; two or more pieces from a single book, 4.5.10.

4.4.4. Title of the book

In general, follow the recommendations for titles given in 2.5. State the full title of the book, including any subtitle. If a book has both a title and a subtitle, put a colon directly after the title, unless the title itself ends in a punctuation mark (e.g., a question mark, an exclamation mark, or a period), and skip a space before giving the subtitle. Place a period after the entire title (the title and any subtitle) unless it ends in a punctuation mark, and skip two spaces before beginning the next item. In underlining the title, include all punctuation *within* the title but not the period at the end (unless it is part of the title).

Extremely long titles or titles usually condensed may be shortened. In shortening a title, always include the beginning words of the title up to the first noun and the words by which the work is customarily known. Indicate any omissions by three spaced periods, four if the omission is at the end of the title (see 2.6.4 on ellipsis). For example, *The Fortunes and Misfortunes of the Famous Moll Flanders* may be cited as

The Fortunes . . . of . . . Moll Flanders.

Likewise, *A Lamentable Tragedie, Mixed Full of Plesant Mirth, Containing the Life of Cambises, King of Percia, from the Beginning of His Kingdome, vnto His Death, His One Good Deede of Execution, after That Many Wicked Deedes and*

Tyrannous Murders, Committed by and through Him, and Last of All, His Odious Death by Gods Iustice Appointed may be cited as

A Lamentable Tragedie . . . of Cambises. . . .

When the title introduces its subtitle as an alternative title (usually by *or*), separate the two by a colon, capitalize the conjunction and follow it by a comma, and capitalize the next word.

"Criticulture: Or, Why We Need at Least Three Criticisms at

     the Present Time."

4.4.5.   Name of editor, translator, or compiler

If the name of an editor, translator, or compiler appears on the title page, it is usually appropriate to include it after the title of the work (see 4.5.12–13). To cite writers of introductions, prefaces, forewords, and afterwords, see 4.5.9.

4.4.6.   Edition used

A book that gives no edition number or name on its title page is probably a first edition, as your reader will assume if your bibliographic entry does not indicate otherwise. If, however, you are using a later edition of a work, identify it in your entry by number (e.g., 2nd ed., 3rd ed., or 4th ed.), by name (e.g., Rev. ed.), or by year (e.g., 1984 ed.)—whichever the title page indicates. Works revised on an annual or other regular basis commonly designate successive editions by year (see 4.5.15).

4.4.7.   Number of volumes

In citing a multivolume work, always state the complete number of volumes (see 4.5.11).

4.4.8.   Name of the series

In citing a book that is part of a publication series, give the name of the series and the arabic numeral denoting the work's place in the series (see 4.5.18).

4.4.9.   Place of publication, publisher, and date of publication

Give the city of publication, the publisher's name, and the year of pub-lication (for a few exceptions, see 4.5.15 and 4.5.24–25). Take these facts directly from the book itself, not from a source such as a bibliography or a library catalog. Publication information usually appears on the title page, the copyright page (i.e., the reverse of the title page), or, particu-larly in books published outside the United States, the colophon at the back of the book. Use a colon and a space between the place of publica-tion and the publisher, a comma and a space between the publisher and the date, and a period after the date.

Since the city of publication is sometimes needed to identify a book, it should always be given. If several cities are listed for the publisher, give only the first. For cities outside the United States, add an abbreviation of the country (or province for cities in Canada) if the name of the city may be ambiguous or unfamiliar to your readers: Manchester, Eng.; Sher-brooke, PQ (see 6.3 for abbreviations of geographical names). To cite the city of publication for a book published in a language other than English, see 4.5.22. If no place of publication is given, write "N.p." for "no place" (see 4.5.25).

Use an appropriately shortened form of the publisher's name, follow-ing the guidelines in 6.5. To cite a work issued under a publisher's special imprint, give the imprint and add the publisher's name after a hyphen: Anchor-Doubleday (see 4.5.19). If the title page indicates that two pub-lishers have brought out the work simultaneously, give both (see 4.5.20). You may omit the name of a publisher for a work published before 1900. If no publisher is given for a later work, write "n.p." for "no publisher" after the colon (see 4.5.25); if a work is privately printed, write "privately printed" (see 4.5.27).

After the publisher's name, a comma, and a space, write the year in which the book was published. If this date is not recorded on the title or copyright page or in the colophon, use the latest copyright date. If the copyright page indicates that the work has had several printings (or "impressions") by the same publisher, use the original publication date. But in citing a new or revised edition, give the date of that edition, not the original date. If you are listing a reprint by a different publisher — for instance, a paperback reprint of a book originally published in a clothbound edition — give the dates of both the original edition and the reprint (see 4.5.14). In citing a multivolume work published over a number of years, give the inclusive dates (see 4.5.11). If no date of publication is printed in the book, write "n.d." or supply the date in square brackets (see 4.5.25).

4.4.10. Page numbers

Give the inclusive page numbers when you cite part of a book (e.g., an essay, short story, or preface). Be sure to give the page numbers of the *entire* piece, not just the pages for the material you have used; specific page references will appear, in parentheses, within the text (see ch. 5). Inclusive page numbers, usually without any identifying abbreviation, follow the publication date, a period, and two spaces (see 4.5.8). For a multivolume work, the page numbers should follow the volume number, a colon, and a space (see 4.5.11). If the book has no pagination, you may indicate "N. pag." as part of the entry (see 4.5.25). When appropriate, the total pagination of a book may be included in the list of works cited: xvi + 269 pp.

4.4.11. Supplementary bibliographic information and annotation

Add, if necessary or desired, supplementary bibliographic data, such as information about additional volumes of a multivolume work (see 4.5.11) or the original version of a translated work (see 4.5.13). Any other annotation or supplementary information appears at the end of the entry.

4.5. Sample entries: Books

The following examples illustrate the recommendations in 4.4.

4.5.1. A book by a single author

To cite a book by a single author, follow the general pattern outlined in 4.4: author's name (reversed for alphabetizing), title (including any subtitle), and publication information (city of publication, publisher, date of publication).

Clark, Kenneth. What Is a Masterpiece? London: Thames, 1979.

Maini, Darshan Dingh. Studies in Punjabi Poetry. New Delhi:

    Vikas, 1979.

Pollak, Vivian R. Dickinson: The Anxiety of Gender. Ithaca:

    Cornell UP, 1984.

4.5.2. An anthology or a compilation

To cite an anthology or a compilation (e.g., a bibliography), record first the name of the editor or compiler, followed by a comma, a space, and the abbreviation "ed." or "comp." If the person has performed more than one function — serving, say, as editor and translator — give both roles.

Nichols, Fred J., ed. and trans. An Anthology of Neo-Latin

    Poetry. New Haven: Yale UP, 1979.

Seller, Maxine Schwartz, ed. Ethnic Theater in the United

    States. Westport: Greenwood, 1983.

Stratman, Carl J., comp. and ed. Bibliography of English

    Printed Tragedy, 1565-1900. Carbondale: Southern

    Illinois UP, 1966.

See also the sections on works in an anthology (4.5.8), introductions and prefaces to books (4.5.9), editions (4.5.12), and translations (4.5.13).

4.5.3.   Two or more books by the same person

In citing two or more books by the same person, give the name in the first entry only. Thereafter, in place of the name, type three hyphens and a period, skip two spaces, and give the title. The three hyphens always stand for exactly the same name(s) as in the preceding entry. If the person named served as editor, translator, or compiler of any of the books, place a comma (not a period) after the three hyphens, skip a space, and write the appropriate abbreviation (ed., trans., or comp.) before giving the title. If the same person served as, say, the editor of two or more works listed consecutively, the abbreviation "ed." must be repeated with each entry. This sort of label, however, does not affect the order in which entries appear; works listed under the same name(s) are alphabetized by title.

Borroff, Marie. Language and the Past: Verbal Artistry in

Frost, Stevens, and Moore. Chicago: U of Chicago P,

1979.

---, trans. Sir Gawain and the Green Knight. New York:

Norton, 1967.

---, ed. Wallace Stevens: A Collection of Critical Essays.

Englewood Cliffs: Prentice, 1963.

Poulet, Georges. Benjamin Constant par lui-même. Paris:

Seuil, 1968.

---, ed. Les chemins actuels de la critique. Paris: Plon,

1967.

---. La poésie éclatée: Baudelaire-Rimbaud. Paris: PUF,

1980.

4.5.4.   A book by two or more persons

In citing a book by two or more persons, give their names in the order in which they appear on the title page—not necessarily in alphabetical

order. Reverse only the name of the first author, add a comma, and give
the other name(s) in normal order: Wellek, René, and Austin Warren.
Place a period after the last name, skip two spaces, and begin the next
item. Even if the authors have the same last name, state each name in
full: Durant, Will, and Ariel Durant. For works with more than three
authors, name only the first and add "et al." ("and others"). If your references are to other than the author named first, you may give more than
the first author (but always begin the entry with the name of the author
listed first on the title page). If the persons named on the title page are
editors, translators, or compilers, place a comma (not a period) after the
last name and add the appropriate abbreviation (eds., trans., or comps.).

Blocker, Clyde E., Robert H. Plummer, and Richard C.

     Richardson, Jr. The Two-Year College: A Social

     Synthesis. Englewood Cliffs: Prentice, 1965.

Bondanella, Peter, and Julia Conaway Bondanella, eds.

     Dictionary of Italian Literature. Westport: Greenwood,

     1979.

Edens, Walter, et al., eds. Teaching Shakespeare. Princeton:

     Princeton UP, 1977.

Janaro, Richard Paul, and Thelma C. Altshuler. The Art of

     Being Human: The Humanities as a Technique for Living.

     2nd ed. New York: Harper, 1984.

Sauerberg, Lars Ole, et al. The Practice of Literary

     Criticism. Odense: Odense UP, 1983.

If a single author cited in an entry is also the first of multiple authors
in the following entry, repeat the name in full; do not substitute three
hyphens. Since the three hyphens always stand for exactly the same
name(s) as in the preceding entry, you have to repeat the name in full
whenever you cite the same person as part of a different authorship.

Knoepflmacher, U. C. Religious Humanism and the Victorian

  Novel: George Eliot, Walter Pater, and Samuel Butler.

  Princeton: Princeton UP, 1970.

Knoepflmacher, U. C., and G. B. Tennyson, eds. Nature and the

  Victorian Imagination. Berkeley: U of California P,

  1977.

Tennyson, G. B., ed. An Introduction to Drama. New York:

  Holt, 1967.

---. Victorian Devotional Poetry: The Tractarian Mode.

  Cambridge: Harvard UP, 1981.

Tennyson, G. B., and Edward Ericson, Jr., eds. Religion and

  Modern Literature: Essays in Theory and Criticism. Grand

  Rapids: Eerdmans, 1975.

Tennyson, G. B., and Donald Gray, eds. Victorian Literature:

  Prose. New York: Macmillan, 1976.

4.5.5. Two or more books by the same multiple authors

In citing two or more works by the same multiple authors, give the
names of the authors in the first entry only. Thereafter, in place of the
names, type three hyphens followed by a period, skip two spaces, and
give the next title. The three hyphens always stand for exactly the same
name(s) as in the preceding entry.

Durant, Will. The Age of Faith. New York: Simon, 1950. Vol.

  4 of The Story of Civilization. 11 vols. 1935-75.

---. Our Oriental Heritage. New York: Simon, 1935. Vol. 1

  of The Story of Civilization. 11 vols. 1935-75.

Durant, Will, and Ariel Durant. The Age of Voltaire. New

    York: Simon, 1965. Vol. 9 of The Story of Civilization.

    11 vols. 1935-75.

---. A Dual Autobiography. New York: Simon, 1977.

---. Rousseau and Romanticism. New York: Simon, 1967. Vol.

    10 of The Story of Civilization. 11 vols. 1935-75.

4.5.6.   A book by a corporate author

In general, cite the book by the corporate author, even if the corporate author is the publisher; if you are citing many books by the same corporate author, you may list them by title and write "By" and the name of the corporate author. (On citing government publications, see 4.5.17.)

American Council on Education. Annual Report, 1970.

    Washington: Amer. Council on Educ., 1971.

Carnegie Council on Policy Studies in Higher Education.

    Giving Youth a Better Chance: Options for Education,

    Work, and Service. San Francisco: Jossey, 1980.

Commission on the Humanities. The Humanities in American

    Life: Report of the Commission on the Humanities.

    Berkeley: U of California P, 1980.

National Committee on Careers for Older Americans. Older

    Americans: An Untapped Resource. Washington: Acad. for

    Educ. Dev., 1979.

4.5.7.   An anonymous book

If a book has no author's name on the title page, do not use either "Anonymous" or "Anon." Begin the entry with the title and alphabetize by the first word other than a definite or indefinite article. (In the sample entries note that *A Handbook of Korea* is alphabetized under "h.")

<u>Dictionary of Ancient Greek Civilization</u>. London: Methuen,

1966.

<u>A Handbook of Korea</u>. 4th ed. Seoul: Korean Overseas

Information Service, Ministry of Culture and Information,

1982.

<u>Literary Market Place: The Directory of American Book

Publishing</u>. 1984 ed. New York: Bowker, 1983.

<u>The Times Atlas of the World</u>. 5th ed. New York: New York

Times, 1975.

4.5.8.   A work in an anthology

First, state the author and title of the piece you are citing (e.g., an essay, a short story, or a poem), normally enclosing the title in quotation marks but underlining instead if the work was originally published as a book (e.g., a play or a novel; see sample entries for "Hansberry" and "Unamuno y Jugo"). If the anthology contains works by different translators, give the translator's name next, preceded by the abbreviation "Trans." (see entry for "Unamuno y Jugo") and followed by the title of the anthology (underlined). If all the works have the same translator or if the collection has an editor, write "Trans." or "Ed." (or "Ed. and trans.") after the title and give that person's name. Cite the inclusive pages for the piece at the end of the citation, after the year of publication, a period, and two spaces.

Auerbach, Erich. "Odysseus' Scar." <u>Mimesis: The

Representation of Reality in Western Literature</u>. Trans.

Willard R. Trask. Princeton: Princeton UP, 1953. 3-23.

García Márquez, Gabriel. "A Very Old Man with Enormous

Wings." "Leaf Storm" and Other Stories. Trans. Gregory

Rabassa. New York: Harper, 1972. 105-12.

Gryphius, Andreas. "Abend." The Oxford Book of German Verse.

Ed. E. L. Stahl. 3rd ed. Oxford: Clarendon, 1967. 48-

49.

Hansberry, Lorraine. A Raisin in the Sun. Black Theater: A

Twentieth-Century Collection of the Work of Its Best

Playwrights. Ed. Lindsay Patterson. New York: Dodd,

1971. 221-76.

Unamuno y Jugo, Miguel de. Abel Sanchez. Trans. Anthony

Kerrigan. Eleven Modern Short Novels. Ed. Leo Hamalian

and Edmond L. Volpe. 2nd ed. New York: Putnam's, 1970.

253-350.

In citing an article or essay in a collection of previously published works, give the complete data for the earlier publication and then add "Rpt. in" ("Reprinted in"), the title of the collection, and the new publication facts. (If you cite the original, not the reprint, in the text and are giving the reprint information for the convenience of your readers, enclose it within parentheses.)

Hamilton, Marie Padgett. "The Meaning of the Middle English

Pearl." PMLA 70 (1955): 805-24. Rpt. in Middle English

Survey: Critical Essays. Ed. Edward Vasta. Notre Dame:

U of Notre Dame P, 1965. 117-45.

Wright, G. Ernest. "What Archaeology Can and Cannot Do."

Biblical Archaeologist 34 (1971): 70-76. (Rpt. in The

Bible in Its Literary Milieu. Ed. John Maier and Vincent

Tollers. Grand Rapids: Eerdmans, 1979. 166-72.)

If a new title has been assigned to the piece, give the original title as well as the original publication information, followed by "Rpt. as" ("Reprinted as") and the new title and publication facts.

Lewis, C. S. "The Anthropological Approach." English and

   Medieval Studies Presented to J. R. R. Tolkien on the

   Occasion of His Seventieth Birthday. Ed. Norman Davis

   and C. L. Wrenn. London: Allen, 1962. 219-23. Rpt. as

   "Viewpoints: C. S. Lewis." Twentieth Century

   Interpretations of Sir Gawain and the Green Knight. Ed.

   Denton Fox. Englewood Cliffs: Prentice, 1968. 100-01.

If you refer to more than one piece from the same collection, you may wish to cross-reference each citation to a single entry for the book itself (see 4.5.10). On citing introductions and prefaces, see 4.5.9. On citing a piece in a multivolume anthology, see 4.5.11.

4.5.9.   An introduction, preface, foreword, or afterword

To cite an introduction, preface, foreword, or afterword, begin with the name of its author and then give the name of the part being cited, capitalized but neither underlined nor put in quotation marks (Introduction, Preface, Foreword, Afterword). The title of the work follows. If the writer of the part cited is different from the author of the complete work, write "By" after the title and cite the author of the work, giving the full name in normal order. If the writer of the piece is also the author of the complete work, use only the last name after "By."

Borges, Jorge Luis. Foreword. Selected Poems, 1923-1967. By

   Borges. Ed. Norman Thomas Di Giovanni. New York: Delta-

   Dell, 1973. xv-xvi.

Doctorow, E. L. Introduction. <u>Sister Carrie</u>. By Theodore

    Dreiser. New York: Bantam, 1982. v-xi.

Johnson, Edgar. Afterword. <u>David Copperfield</u>. By Charles

    Dickens. New York: Signet-NAL, 1962. 871-79.

4.5.10. Cross-references

If you are citing two or more works from the same collection, you may, to avoid unnecessary repetition, list the collection itself, with complete publication information, and cite individual pieces by using cross-references to the main entry. In a cross-reference, the last name of the editor of the collection and the relevant page numbers follow the author's name and the title of the piece.

Chesebro, James W. "Communication, Values, and Popular

    Television Series--A Four-Year Assessment." Newcomb 16-

    54.

De Lauretis, Teresa. "A Semiotic Approach to Television as

    Ideological Apparatus." Newcomb 107-17.

Newcomb, Horace, ed. <u>Television: The Critical View</u>. 2nd ed.

    New York: Oxford UP, 1979.

If you list two or more works under the editor's name, however, add the title (or a shortened version of it) to the cross-reference.

Altieri, Charles. "A Procedural Definition of Literature."

    Hernadi, <u>What Is Literature?</u> 62-78.

Beardsley, Monroe C. "The Name and Nature of Criticism."

    Hernadi, <u>What Is Criticism?</u> 151-61.

Booth, Wayne C. "Criticulture: Or, Why We Need at Least Three

Criticisms at the Present Time." Hernadi, What Is

Criticism? 162-76.

Hernadi, Paul, ed. What Is Criticism? Bloomington: Indiana

UP, 1981.

---, ed. What Is Literature? Bloomington: Indiana UP, 1978.

Hirsch, E. D., Jr. "What Isn't Literature?" Hernadi, What Is

Literature? 24-34.

4.5.11. A multivolume work

In citing a work of two or more volumes, give the total number regardless of the number you use. State this information (e.g., 5 vols.) between the title and the publication information if you are using more than one volume of the work; specific references to volume and page numbers (e.g., 3: 212-13) belong in the text. (See ch. 5 for parenthetical documentation.)

If the volumes of the work were published over a period of years, give the inclusive dates at the end of the citation (e.g., 1952-70). If the work is still in progress, write "to date" after the number of volumes (e.g., 3 vols. to date) and leave a space after the hyphen that follows the beginning date (e.g., 1982- .).

When citing a piece in a multivolume anthology, give the inclusive page number(s) after the publication information for the volume you are citing (see sample entry for "Leopardi").

If you use only one volume of a multivolume work, include the volume number in the bibliographic entry; then you need give only page numbers when you cite that work in the text. If the volume is part of a work that does not assign titles to individual volumes, give the publication information for the volume you are citing. Conclude the entry with the number of volumes for the entire work and, if the volumes were published over a period of years, the inclusive dates of publication (see sample entries for "Daiches" and "Gracián"). If the volume has an individual title, give that title after the author's name, add a period, and give the publication information for the volume. Next cite the volume number, preceded by "Vol." and followed by the word "of," the title of the complete work, the total number of volumes, and, if the work appeared over a period of years, the inclusive publication dates (see sample entry for "Churchill").

Churchill, Winston S. <u>The Age of Revolution</u>. New York: Dodd,

   1957. Vol. 3 of <u>A History of the English-Speaking</u>

   <u>Peoples</u>. 4 vols. 1956-58.

Daiches, David. <u>A Critical History of English Literature</u>.

   2nd ed. Vol. 2. New York: Ronald, 1970. 2 vols.

Gracián, Baltasar. <u>El criticón</u>. Ed. M. Romera-Navarro. Vol.

   2. Philadelphia: U of Pennsylvania P, 1939. 3 vols.

   1938-40.

Inge, M. Thomas, Maurice Duke, and Jackson R. Bryer, eds.

   <u>Black American Writers: Bibliographical Essays</u>. 2 vols.

   New York: St. Martin's, 1978.

Leopardi, Giacomo. "L'infinito." <u>Poesie-Prose</u>. Ed. Giovanni

   Ferretti. Vol. 1. Torino: UTET, 1966. 94. 2 vols.

   1966-68.

Potter, G. R., et al. <u>The New Cambridge Modern History</u>. 14

   vols. Cambridge: Cambridge UP, 1957-70.

Schlesinger, Arthur M., gen. ed. <u>History of U.S. Political</u>

   <u>Parties</u>. 4 vols. New York: Chelsea, 1973.

Wing, Donald, et al., eds. <u>Short-Title Catalogue of Books</u>

   <u>Printed in England, Scotland, Ireland, Wales, and British</u>

   <u>America and of English Books Printed in Other Countries,</u>

   <u>1641-1700</u>. 2nd ed. 2 vols. to date. New York: MLA,

   1972- .

4.5.12. An "edition"

Every published book is, in one sense, an "edition." Here, however, the term designates a work attributed not only to an author or authors but also to an editor who has made substantive contributions to the contents. To cite an edition, begin with the author if you refer primarily to the text itself; give the editor's name, preceded by the abbreviation "Ed.," after the title. If the book is a volume of a multivolume work edited by the same person, state the editor's name after the title of the multivolume work (see entry for "Arnold").

Arnold, Matthew. The Last Word. Ann Arbor: U of Michigan P,

1977. Vol. 11 of Complete Prose Works of Matthew Arnold.

Ed. R. H. Super. 11 vols. 1960-77.

Chaucer, Geoffrey. The Works of Geoffrey Chaucer. Ed. F. N.

Robinson. 2nd ed. Boston: Houghton, 1957.

If you cite more than one volume of a multivolume work, give one listing for the entire work. Parenthetical references in the text will document the specific volumes you use (see ch. 5).

Dewey, John. The Early Works, 1882-1898. Ed. Jo Ann

Boydston. 4 vols. Carbondale: Southern Illinois UP,

1967-71.

If your citations of a work are primarily to the editor's contributions (e.g., the introduction or notes or the editing of the text) or if you are citing several different editions of the work of one author, begin the entry with the editor's name followed by a comma and the abbreviation "ed.," write "By" after the title, and give the author's name in full in normal order.

Bowers, Fredson, ed. The Red Badge of Courage: An Episode of

the American Civil War. By Stephen Crane.

Charlottesville: UP of Virginia, 1975. Vol. 2 of The

Works of Stephen Crane. 10 vols. 1969-76.

4.5.13. A translation

In citing a translation, state the author's name first if most of your references are to the work itself and give the translator's name, preceded by "Trans.," after the title. If a work has both an editor and a translator, list them in logical order: usually the translator's name will come first, but list the editor's name first if the translator has translated an edited work.

Dostoevsky, Feodor. Crime and Punishment. Trans. Jessie

Coulson. Ed. George Gibian. New York: Norton, 1964.

Metastasio, Pietro. Three Melodramas. Trans. Joseph G.

Fucilla. Studies in Romance Langs. 24. Lexington: UP of

Kentucky, 1981.

Sastre, Alfonso. Sad Are the Eyes of William Tell. Trans.

Leonard Pronko. The New Wave Spanish Drama. Ed. George

E. Wellwarth. New York: New York UP, 1970. 265-321.

If your citations are to the comments of the translator, or to the translator's decisions in preparing the text, begin the bibliographic entry with the translator's name, followed by a comma and the abbreviation "trans.," write "By" after the title, and give the author's name in full in normal order. (On citing anthologies of translated works by different authors, see 4.5.8.)

Coulson, Jessie, trans. Crime and Punishment. By Feodor

Dostoevsky. Ed. George Gibian. New York: Norton, 1964.

Fucilla, Joseph G., trans. Three Melodramas. By Pietro

Metastasio. Studies in Romance Langs. 24. Lexington: UP

of Kentucky, 1981.

Although not required, some or all of the original publication information may be added at the end of the entry.

Ducrot, Oswald, and Tzvetan Todorov. Encyclopedic Dictionary

of the Sciences of Language. Trans. Catherine Porter.

Baltimore: Johns Hopkins UP, 1979. Trans. of

Dictionnaire encyclopédique des sciences du langage.

Paris: Seuil, 1972.

Salinas, Pedro. My Voice because of You. Trans. Willis

Barnstone. Albany: State U of New York P, 1976. Trans.

of La voz a ti debida. 1933.

4.5.14. A republished book

In citing a republished book—for example, a paperback version of a book originally published in a clothbound version—give the original publication date, followed by a period and two spaces, before the publication information for the book you are citing.

Doctorow, E. L. Welcome to Hard Times. 1960. New York:

Bantam, 1976.

Malamud, Bernard. The Natural. 1952. New York: Avon, 1980.

Mead, Margaret. Blackberry Winter: My Earlier Years. 1972.

New York: Pocket, 1975.

Although not required, additional information pertaining to the original publication may precede the original publication date.

Willey, Basil. The Eighteenth Century Background: Studies on

the Idea of Nature in the Thought of the Period. London:

Chatto, 1940. Boston: Beacon, 1961.

If the republication adds new material, such as an introduction, include the information after the original publication facts.

Dreiser, Theodore. <u>Sister Carrie</u>. 1900. Introd. E. L.

    Doctorow. New York: Bantam, 1982.

4.5.15. An article in a reference book

Treat an encyclopedia article or a dictionary entry as you would a piece in a collection (4.5.8), but do not cite the editor of the reference work. If the article is signed, give the author first (often articles in reference books are signed with initials identified elsewhere in the work); if it is unsigned, give the title first. If the encyclopedia or dictionary arranges articles alphabetically, you may omit volume and page numbers.

When citing familiar reference books, especially those that frequently appear in new editions, do not give full publication information. For such works, list only the edition (if stated) and the year of publication.

"Azimuthal Equidistant Projection." <u>Webster's New Collegiate</u>

    <u>Dictionary</u>. 1980 ed.

Chiappini, Luciano. "Este, House of." <u>Encyclopaedia</u>

    <u>Britannica: Macropaedia</u>. 1974.

"Graham, Martha." <u>Who's Who of American Women</u>. 13th ed.

    1983-84.

"Mandarin." <u>Encyclopedia Americana</u>. 1980 ed.

When citing less familiar reference books, however, especially those that have appeared in only one edition, give full publication information.

Brakeley, Theresa C. "Mourning Songs." <u>Funk and Wagnalls</u>

    <u>Standard Dictionary of Folklore, Mythology, and Legend</u>.

    Ed. Maria Leach and Jerome Fried. 2 vols. New York:

    Crowell, 1950.

Trainen, Isaac N., et al. "Religious Directives in Medical

Ethics." Encyclopedia of Bioethics. Ed. Warren T.

Reich. 4 vols. New York: Free, 1978.

4.5.16. A pamphlet

Treat a pamphlet as you would a book.

Kefauver, Weldon A., ed. Scholars and Their Publishers. New

York: MLA, 1977.

Kilgus, Robert. Color Scripsit Program Manual. Fort Worth:

Tandy, 1981.

4.5.17. A government publication

Because government publications emanate from many sources, they present special problems in bibliographic citation. In general, if the writer of the document is not known, treat the government agency as the author—that is, state the name of the government first, followed by the name of the agency, using an abbreviation if the context makes it clear. (But see below for citing a document whose author is known.) If you are citing two or more works issued by the same government, substitute three hyphens for the name in each entry after the first. If you cite more than one work by the same government agency, each subsequent entry should show three hyphens in place of the government and three additional hyphens in place of the agency.

California. Dept. of Industrial Relations.

United States. Cong. House.

---. ---. Senate.

---. Dept. of Health and Human Services.

The title of the publication, underlined, should follow immediately. In citing a congressional document other than the *Congressional Record* (which requires only a date and a page number), include such information as the number and session of Congress, the house (S or HR), and the type and number of the publication. Types of congressional publications include bills (S 33; HR 77), resolutions (S. Res. 20; H. Res. 50), reports (S. Rept. 9; H. Rept. 142), and documents (S. Doc. 333; H. Doc. 222). The usual publishing information comes next (i.e., place, publisher, and date). Most federal publications, whatever branch of government produces them, are published by the Government Printing Office (GPO) in Washington, DC; its British counterpart is Her (or His) Majesty's Stationery Office (HMSO) in London. Documents issued by the United Nations and most local governments, however, do not emanate from a central office; give the publishing information that appears on the title page.

Cong. Rec. 7 Feb. 1973: 3831-51.

Great Britain. Ministry of Defence. Author and Subject

Catalogues of the Naval Library, Ministry of Defence. 5

vols. London: HMSO, 1967.

New York State. Committee on State Prisons. Investigation of

the New York State Prisons. 1883. New York: Arno, 1974.

United Nations. Centre for National Resources. State

Petroleum Enterprises in Developing Countries. Elmsford:

Pergamon, 1980.

---. Economic Commission for Africa. Industrial Growth in

Africa. New York: United Nations, 1963.

United States. Cong. Joint Committee on the Investigation of

the Pearl Harbor Attack. Hearings. 79th Cong., 1st and

2nd sess. 32 vols. Washington: GPO, 1946.

---. ---. Senate. Subcommittee on Constitutional Amendments

of the Committee on the Judiciary. Hearings on the

"Equal Rights" Amendment. 91st Cong., 2nd sess. S. Res.

61. Washington: GPO, 1970.

---. Dept. of Labor. Bureau of Statistics. Dictionary of

Occupational Titles. 4th ed. Washington: GPO, 1977.

---. Dept. of State. Office of Public Affairs. Korea, 1945-

1947: A Report on Political Development and Economic

Resources. 1948. Westport: Greenwood, 1968.

If you cite a government document with a known author, you may either give the name first in the entry or, if you list the agency first, place it after "By," in normal order, following the title.

Washburne, E. B. Memphis Riots and Massacres. U. S. 39th

Cong., 2nd sess. H. Rept. 101. 1866. New York: Arno,

1969.

or

United States. Cong. House. Memphis Riots and Massacres.

By E. B. Washburne. 39th Cong., 2nd sess. H. Rept. 101.

1866. New York: Arno, 1969.

4.5.18. A book in a series

If the title page or the preceding page (the half-title page) indicates that the book you are citing is part of a series, include the series name, neither underlined nor enclosed in quotation marks, and the series number, followed by a period, before the publishing information.

Curtius, Ernst Robert. European Literature and the Latin

Middle Ages. Trans. Willard Trask. Bollingen Series 36.

Princeton: Princeton UP, 1953.

Kellman, Steven G., ed. <u>Approaches to Teaching Camus's</u> The

    Plague. Approaches to Teaching Masterpieces of World

    Literature 6. New York: MLA, 1985.

Silver, Isidore. <u>Ronsard and the Grecian Lyre</u>. Travaux

    d'humanisme et Renaissance 12. Genève: Droz, 1981.

4.5.19. A publisher's imprint

If the title page or copyright page includes the name of a publisher's special imprint, give the publisher's name after the imprint name and a hyphen (e.g., Anchor-Doubleday, Belknap-Harvard UP, Delacorte-Dell, Mentor-NAL). The name of a publisher's imprint often appears above the publisher's name on the title page.

Hsu, Kai-yu, ed. and trans. <u>Twentieth-Century Chinese Poetry</u>.

    Garden City: Anchor-Doubleday, 1964.

Tolstoy, Leo. <u>The Kingdom of God Is within You</u>. Trans.

    Constance Garnett. Lincoln: Bison-U of Nebraska P, 1984.

4.5.20. A book with multiple publishers

If the title page lists two or more publishers — not just two or more offices of the same publisher — include both, in the order given, as part of the publication information, putting a semicolon after the name of the first publisher.

Duff, J. Wight. <u>A Literary History of Rome: From the Origins</u>

    <u>to the Close of the Golden Age</u>. Ed. A. M. Duff. 3rd ed.

    1953. London: Benn; New York: Barnes, 1967.

Shelley, Percy Bysshe. <u>Selected Poems</u>. Ed. Timothy Webb.

    London: Dent; Totowa: Rowman, 1977.

4.5.21. Published proceedings of a conference

Treat the published proceedings of a conference as you would a book, but add pertinent information about the conference (unless the book title includes such information).

Gordon, Alan M., and Evelyn Rugg, eds. Actas del Sexto

Congreso Internacional de Hispanistas celebrado en

Toronto del 22 al 26 agosto de 1977. Toronto: Dept. of

Spanish and Portuguese, U of Toronto, 1980.

Humanistic Scholarship in America. Proc. of a Conference on

the Princeton Studies in the Humanities. 5-6 Nov. 1965.

Princeton: Princeton U, 1966.

When citing a particular presentation in the proceedings, treat it as a work in a collection of pieces by different authors (see 4.5.8).

4.5.22. A book in a language other than English

In citing a book published in a language other than English, give all information exactly as it appears on the title or copyright page or in the colophon. Provide translations, in brackets, of the title and the city of publication if clarifications seem necessary for your audience (e.g., Et dukkehjem [A Doll House]; Wien [Vienna]). Or you may substitute the English name of a foreign city. Use appropriate abbreviations for publishers' names (see 6.5). (For capitalization in languages other than English, see 2.4.2–9.)

Dahlhaus, Carl. Musikästhetik. Köln: Gerig, 1967.

Gramsci, Antonio. Gli intelletuali e l'organizzazione della

cultura. Torino: Einaudi, 1949.

Rey-Flaud, Henri. Pour une dramaturgie du Moyen Age. Paris:

PUF, 1980.

Wachowicz, Barbara. <u>Marie jeho života</u>. Praha [Prague]:

Lidové, 1979.

4.5.23. A book with a title within its title

If the book title you are citing contains a title normally enclosed within quotation marks (e.g., a short story or a poem), retain the quotation marks and underline the entire title. If the closing quotation mark appears at the end of the title, place a period before the quotation mark. If the book title you are citing contains a title normally underlined (e.g., a novel or a play), the shorter title is neither placed in quotation marks nor underlined; it appears, instead, in "roman type" — that is, not underlined.

Danzig, Allan, ed. <u>Twentieth Century Interpretations of "The</u>

<u>Eve of St. Agnes."</u> Englewood Cliffs: Prentice, 1971.

Dunn, Richard J. David Copperfield<u>: An Annotated</u>

<u>Bibliography</u>. New York: Garland, 1981.

Fielding, Henry. Joseph Andrews <u>and</u> Shamela. Ed. Martin C.

Battestin. Boston: Houghton, 1961.

Mades, Leonard. <u>The Armor and the Brocade: A Study of</u> Don

Quijote <u>and</u> The Courtier. New York: Las Americas, 1968.

4.5.24. A book published before 1900

When citing a book published before 1900, you may omit the name of the publisher.

Dewey, John. <u>The Study of Ethics: A Syllabus</u>. Ann Arbor,

1894.

Udall, John. <u>The Combate between Christ and the Devil: Four</u>

<u>Sermones on the Temptations of Christ</u>. London, 1589.

4.5.25. A book without stated publication information or pagination

When a book does not indicate the publisher, the place or date of publication, or the pagination, supply as much of the missing data as you can, enclosing the information in brackets to show that it did not come from the source:

New York: U of Gotham P, [1983].

If the date can only be approximated, put it after a "c." (for "circa" 'around'; e.g., [c. 1983]). If you are uncertain about the accuracy of the information you are supplying, add a question mark (e.g., [1983?]). When you can supply very little information, add the name of the library and the shelfmark or call numbers of the copy you are citing. If you can provide no information, use the following abbreviations:

n.p.	no place of publication given
n.p.	no publisher given
n.d.	no date of publication given
n. pag.	no pagination given

Inserted before the colon, the abbreviation "n.p." indicates "no place"; after the colon it indicates "no publisher." "N. pag." informs your reader why no page references for the work are included in your citations.

No date

New York: U of Gotham P, n.d.

No pagination

New York: U of Gotham P, 1983. N. pag.

No place

N.p.: U of Gotham P, 1983.

No publisher

New York: n.p., 1983.

Neither place nor publisher

N.p.: n.p., 1983.

Malachi, Zvi, ed. <u>Proceedings of the International Conference</u>

on Literary and Linguistic Computing. [Tel Aviv]: [Tel

Aviv U Fac. of Humanities], n.d.

<u>Photographic View Album of Cambridge</u>. [England]: n.p., n.d.

N. pag.

4.5.26. An unpublished dissertation

In citing the unpublished version of a dissertation, place the title in quotation marks; do not underline it. Then write the descriptive label "Diss.," preceded and followed by two spaces, and add the name of the degree-granting university, followed by a comma, a space, and the year.

Boyle, Anthony T. "The Epistemological Evolution of

Renaissance Utopian Literature: 1516-1657." Diss. New

York U, 1983.

Johnson, Nancy Kay. "Cultural and Psychosocial Determinants

of Health and Illness." Diss. U of Washington, 1980.

For citing a dissertation abstract published in *Dissertation Abstracts* or *Dissertation Abstracts International*, see 4.7.12. For documenting other unpublished writing, see 4.8.15.

4.5.27. A published dissertation

Treat a published dissertation as you would a book, but add pertinent dissertation information and, if the work has been published by University Microfilms International (UMI), the order number.

Brewda, Lee Aaron. A Semantically-Based Verb Valence Analysis

of Old Saxon. Diss. Princeton U, 1981. Ann Arbor: UMI,

1982. 8203236.

Dietze, Rudolf F. Ralph Ellison: The Genesis of an Artist.

Diss. U Erlangen-Nürnberg, 1982. Erlanger Beiträge zur

Sprach- und Kunstwissenschaft 70. Nürnberg: Carl, 1982.

Wendriner, Karl Georg. Der Einfluss von Goethes Wilhelm

Meister auf das Drama der Romantiker. Diss. U Bonn,

1907. Leipzig: privately printed, 1907.

4.6. Citing articles in periodicals: Information required

4.6.1. General guidelines

An entry for an article in a periodical, like an entry for a book, has three main divisions: author, title of the article, and publication information. For scholarly journals, publication information generally includes the journal title, volume number, the year of publication, and inclusive page numbers.

Booth, Wayne C. "Kenneth Burke's Way of Knowing." Critical

Inquiry 1 (1974): 1-22.

Sometimes, however, additional information is required. In citing articles in periodicals, normally arrange the information in the following order:

1. Author's name
2. Title of the article
3. Name of the periodical
4. Series number or name
5. Volume number
6. Date of publication
7. Page numbers

Each of these items of information is discussed in general terms in 4.6.2–8, and examples of the recommendations are given in 4.7.

4.6.2.   Author's name

Take the author's name from the first page or the last page of the article and follow the recommendations for citing names of authors of books (4.4.2).

4.6.3.   Title of the article

Give the title of the article in full, enclosed in quotation marks (not underlined). Unless the title has its own concluding punctuation (e.g., a question mark), put a period before the closing quotation mark. Follow the recommendations for titles given in 2.5.

4.6.4.   Name of the periodical

When citing a periodical, omit any introductory article but otherwise give the name, underlined, as it appears on the title page: *William and Mary Quarterly* (not *The William and Mary Quarterly*). Give the city or institution in square brackets to locate an unfamiliar journal or to distinguish a periodical from another with the same name. For newspaper titles, see 4.7.6.

4.6.5.   Series number or name

If you list a periodical that has appeared in more than one series, state the number or name of the series after the journal title (see 4.7.3).

4.6.6.   Volume number

Do not write "volume" or "vol." before the volume number. Although published several times a year (usually four), most scholarly journals use continuous pagination throughout each annual volume (see 4.7.1). Some periodicals, however, page issues independently; others use issue numbers alone and do not have volume numbers (see 4.7.2).

4.6.7.   Date of publication

Leave a space after the volume number and give the year of publication, in parentheses, followed by a colon, a space, and the inclusive page numbers of the article.

College Literature 8 (1981): 85-87.

In citing daily, weekly, or monthly periodicals, omit volume and issue numbers and give the complete date instead, followed by a colon, a space, and the page number(s). Abbreviate all months except May, June, and July.

Folio Jan. 1980: 29-31.

Publishers Weekly 19 Feb. 1982: 6-7.

For editions of newspapers, see 4.7.6.

4.6.8.   Page numbers

Using the rules for writing inclusive numbers (see 2.7.6), give the pages for the complete article, not just the pages used. (Specific page references appear parenthetically at appropriate places in your text; see ch. 5.) Give the page reference for the first page exactly as it appears in the source: 198-232, A32-34, 28/WETA-29, lxii-lxv. A period follows the page numbers, concluding the entry. When an article is not printed on consecutive pages — if, for example, it begins on page 6, then skips to page 10, and continues on page 22 — write only the first page number and a plus sign, leaving no intervening space (e.g., 6+).

Hook, Janet. "Raise Standards of Admission, Colleges Urged."

Chronicle of Higher Education 4 May 1983: 1+.

For section numbers of newspapers, see 4.7.6.

4.7.   Sample entries: Articles in periodicals

The following examples illustrate the recommendations in 4.6.

4.7.1.   An article in a journal with continuous pagination

A bibliographic reference to an article in a periodical typically begins with the author's name, the title of the article, and the name of the journal. If the article you are citing appears in a journal with continuous pagination throughout the annual volume (i.e., if the first issue ends on page 130, the next one begins on page 131, etc.), give the volume number followed by the year of publication (in parentheses), a colon, and the inclusive page numbers.

Clark, Herbert H., and Thomas H. Carlson. "Hearers and Speech

Acts." Language 58 (1982): 332-73.

Kauffman, Judith. "Musique et matière romanesque dans

Moderato cantabile de Marguerite Duras." Etudes

littéraires 15 (1982): 97-112.

Ramsey, Jarold W. "The Wife Who Goes Out like a Man, Comes

Back as a Hero: The Art of Two Oregon Indian Narratives."

PMLA 92 (1977): 9-18.

Spear, Karen. "Building Cognitive Skills in Basic Writers."

Teaching English in the Two-Year College 9 (1983): 91-98.

4.7.2.   An article in a journal that pages each issue separately or that uses only issue numbers

For a journal that does not number pages continuously throughout an annual volume but begins each issue on page 1, add a period and the issue number, without any intervening space, directly after the volume number (e.g., 14.2, signifying volume 14, issue 2; 10.3-4, for volume 10, issues 3 and 4 combined).

Barthelme, Frederick. "Architecture." Kansas Quarterly 13.3-4 (1981): 77-80.

Lyon, George Ella. "Contemporary Appalachian Poetry: Sources and Directions." Kentucky Review 2.2 (1981): 3-22.

Monk, Patricia. "Frankenstein's Daughters: The Problems of the Feminine Image in Science Fiction." Mosaic 13.3-4 (1980): 15-27.

In citing a journal that uses only issue numbers, treat the issue number as you would a volume number.

Pritchard, Allan. "West of the Great Divide: A View of the Literature of British Columbia." Canadian Literature 94 (1982): 96-112.

Wilson, Katharina M. "Tertullian's De cultu foeminarum and Utopia." Moreana 73 (1982): 69-74.

4.7.3.   An article from a journal with more than one series

In citing a journal with numbered series, write the number (an arabic digit with the appropriate ordinal suffix: 2nd, 3rd, 4th, etc.) and the abbreviation "ser." between the journal title and the volume number (see sample entry for "Johnson"). For a journal divided into a new series and an original series, indicate the series by "ns" or "os," skip a space, and give the volume number (see sample entry for "Avery").

Avery, Robert. "Foreign Influence on the Nautical Terminology

of Russian in the Eighteenth Century." Oxford Slavonic

Papers ns 14 (1981): 73-92.

Johnson, Michael P. "Runaway Slaves and the Slave Communities

in South Carolina, 1799-1830." William and Mary

Quarterly 3rd ser. 38 (1981): 418-41.

4.7.4. An article from a weekly or biweekly periodical

In citing a periodical published every week or every two weeks, give the complete date (beginning with the day and abbreviating the month, unless it is May, June, or July) instead of the volume and issue numbers.

Begley, Sharon. "A Healthy Dose of Laughter." Newsweek 4

Oct. 1982: 74.

McDonald, Kim. "Space Shuttle Columbia's Weightless

Laboratory Attracts Research." Chronicle of Higher

Education 28 Oct. 1981: 6-7.

Motulsky, Arno G. "Impact of Genetic Manipulation on Society

and Medicine." Science 14 Jan. 1983: 135-40.

4.7.5. An article from a monthly or bimonthly periodical

In citing a periodical published every month or every two months, give the month (abbreviated, unless May, June, or July) and year instead of the volume number and issue.

Corcoran, Elizabeth. "Space and the Arts." <u>Space World</u> Oct.

1982: 14+.

Ratcliffe, Carter. "Where a Visionary Opened His Eyes: A

Fresh Look at El Greco." <u>Saturday Review</u> Mar.-Apr. 1983:

24-27.

Snyder, Mark. "Self-Fulfilling Stereotypes." <u>Psychology</u>

<u>Today</u> July 1982: 60-68.

Tucker, W. Henry. "Dilemma in Teaching Engineering Ethics."

<u>Chemical Engineering Progress</u> Apr. 1983: 20-25.

4.7.6.   An article from a daily newspaper

In citing a daily newspaper, give the name as it appears on the masthead but omit any introductory article: *New York Times* (not *The New York Times*). If the city of publication is not included in the name of the newspaper, add it in square brackets, not underlined, after the name: *Star-Ledger* [Newark, NJ]. Next, give the complete date—day, month (abbreviated, unless May, June, or July), and year—instead of the volume and issue numbers.

Because different editions of newspapers contain different material, specify the edition (if one is given on the masthead), preceded by a comma, after the date:

Collins, Glenn. "Single-Father Survey Finds Adjustment a

Problem." <u>New York Times</u> 21 Nov. 1983, late ed.: B17.

or

Collins, Glenn. "Single-Father Survey Finds Adjustment a

Problem." <u>New York Times</u> 21 Nov. 1983, natl. ed.: 20.

If each section is paginated separately, indicate the appropriate section number or letter. Determining how to indicate a section, however, can sometimes be complicated. The *New York Times*, for example, cur-

rently designates sections in three distinct ways, depending on the day
of the week. On Monday through Friday, there are normally four sections, labeled A, B, C, and D and paginated separately, with each page
number preceded by the section letter (e.g., A1, B1, C5, D3). On Satur-
day, the paper is not divided into specific sections, and pagination is continuous, from the first page to the last. (The daily national edition follows
the same practice.) Finally, the Sunday edition contains several individually paged sections (travel, arts and leisure, book review, business, and
others), designated not by letters but by numbers, which do not appear
as parts of the page numbers. Each system calls for a different method
of indicating section and page.

If the newspaper is not divided into sections, give the page number
after the date (or after the edition if one is stated on the masthead), a
colon, and a space (see sample entry for "Dalin"). If the pagination includes a section designation, give the page number as it appears (e.g.,
C1; see sample entries for "Greenberg" and "Schreiner"). If the section
designation is not part of the pagination, put a comma after the date (or,
if pertinent, the edition) and add the abbreviation "sec.," the appropriate letter or number, a colon, and the page number (see sample entry
for "Kerr").

Dalin, Damon. "A $7 Greeting Card? Yes, but Listen to the

     Melody It Will Play for You." Wall Street Journal 10 May

     1983, eastern ed.: 37.

Greenberg, Daniel S. "Ridding American Politics of Polls."

     Washington Post 16 Sept. 1980: A17.

Kerr, Walter. "When One Inspired Gesture Illuminates the

     Stage." New York Times 8 Jan. 1984, late ed., sec. 2:

     1+.

Schreiner, Tim. "Future Is A) Dim or B) Bright (Pick One)."

     USA Today 2 June 1983: 3A.

4.7.7.   An editorial

If you are citing a signed editorial, begin with the author's name, give
the title, and then add the descriptive label "Editorial," neither under-

lined nor enclosed in quotation marks. Conclude with the appropriate publication information. If the editorial is unsigned, begin with the title and continue in the same way.

```
Malkofsky, Morton.  "Let the Unions Negotiate What's

    Negotiable."  Editorial.  Learning Oct. 1982: 6.

"An Uneasy Silence."  Editorial.  Computerworld 28 Mar. 1983:

    54.
```

4.7.8.   An anonymous article

If no author's name is given for the article you are citing, begin the entry with the title and alphabetize by title.

```
"Portents for Future Learning."  Time 21 Sept. 1981: 65.

"The Starry Sky."  Odyssey Jan. 1984: 26-27.
```

4.7.9.   A letter to the editor

To identify a letter to the editor, write "Letter" after the name of the author, but do not underline the word or place it in quotation marks.

```
Levin, Harry.  Letter.  Partisan Review 47 (1980): 320.
```

If an author has replied to a letter, identify the response as "Reply to letter of . . ." and add the name of the writer of the initial letter. Do not underline this information or place it in quotation marks.

```
Patai, Daphne.  Reply to letter of Erwin Hester.  PMLA 98

    (1983): 257-58.
```

4.7.10. A review

In citing a review, give the reviewer's name and the title of the review (if there is one); then write "Rev. of" (neither underlined nor placed in quotation marks), the title of the work reviewed, a comma, "by," and the name of the author. If the work of an editor or translator is under review, use "ed." or "trans." instead of "by." For the review of a performance, add pertinent information about the production (see sample entry for "Henahan"). Conclude with the name of the periodical and the rest of the publication information.

If the review is titled but unsigned, begin the entry with the title of the review and alphabetize by that title (see sample entry for "The Cooling of an Admiration"). If the review is neither titled nor signed, begin the entry with "Rev. of" and alphabetize under the title of the work being reviewed (see sample entry for *Anthology of Danish Literature*).

Rev. of <u>Anthology of Danish Literature</u>, ed. F. J. Billeskov

  Jansen and P. M. Mitchell. <u>Times Literary Supplement</u> 7

  July 1972: 785.

Ashton, Sherley. Rev. of <u>Death and Dying</u>, by David L. Bender

  and Richard C. Hagen. <u>Humanist</u> July-Aug. 1982: 60.

"The Cooling of an Admiration." Rev. of <u>Pound/Joyce: The</u>

  <u>Letters of Ezra Pound to James Joyce</u>, ed. Forrest Read.

  <u>Times Literary Supplement</u> 6 Mar. 1969: 239-40.

Edwards, R. Dudley. Rev. of <u>The Dissolution of the Religious</u>

  <u>Orders in Ireland under Henry VIII</u>, by Brendan Bradshaw.

  <u>Renaissance Quarterly</u> 29 (1976): 401-03.

Henahan, Donal. Rev. of <u>Rinaldo</u>, by George Frideric Handel.

  Metropolitan Opera, New York. <u>New York Times</u> 21 Jan.

  1984, late ed.: 9.

Updike, John. "Cohn's Doom." Rev. of <u>God's Grace</u>, by Bernard

  Malamud. <u>New Yorker</u> 8 Nov. 1982: 167-70.

4.7.11. An article whose title contains a quotation or a title within quotation marks

If the title of the article you are citing contains a quotation or a title within quotation marks, use single quotation marks around the quotation or the shorter title (see 2.5.4).

Carrier, Warren. "Commonplace Costumes and Essential

    Gaudiness: Wallace Stevens' 'The Emperor of Ice Cream.'"

    College Literature 1 (1974): 230-35.

Duncan-Jones, E. E. "Moore's 'A Kiss à l'Antique' and Keats's

    'Ode on a Grecian Urn.'" Notes and Queries ns 28 (1981):

    316-17.

Nitzsche, Jane Chance. "''As swete as is the roote of lycorys,

    or any cetewale': Herbal Imagery in Chaucer's Miller's

    Tale." Chaucer Newsletter 2.1 (1980): 6-8.

4.7.12. An abstract from *Dissertation Abstracts* or *Dissertation Abstracts International*

Beginning with volume 30 (1969), *Dissertation Abstracts* (*DA*) became *Dissertation Abstracts International* (*DAI*). From volume 27 to volume 36, *DA* and *DAI* were paginated in two series: A for humanities and social sciences, B for the sciences. With volume 37, *DAI* added a third separately paginated section: C for abstracts of European dissertations. Identify the degree-granting institution at the end of a *DA* or *DAI* entry (for citing dissertations themselves, see 4.5.26-27).

Gans, Eric L. "The Discovery of Illusion: Flaubert's Early

    Works, 1835-1837." DA 27 (1967): 3046A. Johns Hopkins

    U.

Johnson, Nancy Kay. "Cultural and Psychosocial Determinants of Health and Illness." <u>DAI</u> 40 (1980): 4235B. U of

Washington.

Norris, Christine Lynn. "Literary Allusion in the Tales of

Isak Dinesen." <u>DAI</u> 43 (1982): 453A. U of California,

San Diego.

Peltzer, U. "Interaktion und Entscheidung." <u>DAI</u> 41 (1981):

901C. U Augsburg.

4.7.13. A serialized article

To cite a serialized article or a series of related articles published in
more than one issue of a periodical, include all bibliographic information in one entry if each installment has the same author and title.

Gillespie, Gerald. "Novella, Nouvelle, Novelle, Short Novel?

A Review of Terms." <u>Neophilologus</u> 51 (1967): 117-27,

225-30.

Meserole, Harrison T., and James M. Rambeau. "Articles on

American Literature Appearing in Current Periodicals."

<u>American Literature</u> 52 (1981): 688-705; 53 (1981): 164-

80, 348-59.

If the installments bear different titles, list each one separately. You may
include a brief description at the end of the entry to indicate that the article is part of a series.

Gottlieb, Martin. "Pressure and Compromise Saved Times Square

Project." <u>New York Times</u> 10 Mar. 1984, late ed.: 25.

Pt. 2 of a series begun on 9 Mar. 1984.

---. "Times Square Development Plan: A Lesson in Politics and

    Power." New York Times 9 Mar. 1984, late ed.: B1. Pt. 1

    of a series.

4.7.14. A special issue of a journal

To cite an entire special issue of a journal, begin the entry with the name of the person who edited the issue (if given on the title page), followed by a comma and the abbreviation "ed." Next give the title of the special issue (underlined). After a period and two spaces, indicate "Spec. issue of" and the name of the journal. Conclude the entry with both the journal's volume number and the issue number (separated by a period: 6.3), the year of publication (in parentheses), a colon, a space, and the complete pagination of the issue. If no special editor's name is given, begin with the title of the issue. If the issue has been republished in book form, add the relevant information (city of publication, publisher, date of publication).

Jahner, Elaine, ed. American Indians Today: Their Thought,

    Their Literature, Their Art. Spec. issue of Book Forum

    5.3 (1981): 309-432.

Mitchell, W. J. T., ed. The Politics of Interpretation.

    Spec. issue of Critical Inquiry 9.1 (1982): 1-278.

    Chicago: U of Chicago P, 1983.

Picaresque Tradition. Spec. issue of College Literature 6.3

    (1979): 165-270.

If you are citing one article from a special issue and wish to indicate complete publication information concerning the issue, use the following form:

Allen, Paula Gunn. "'The Grace That Remains': American Indian

    Women's Literature." American Indians Today: Their

Thought, Their Literature, Their Art. Ed. Elaine Jahner.

Spec. issue of Book Forum 5.3 (1981): 376-82.

4.8.   Sample entries: Other sources

4.8.1.   Computer software

An entry for a commercially produced computer program should contain the following information: the writer of the program, if known; the title of the program, underlined; the descriptive label "Computer software," neither underlined nor enclosed in quotation marks; the distributor; and the year of publication. Put a period after each item except the distributor, which is followed by a comma. At the end of the entry add any other pertinent information—for example, the computer for which the program is designed (e.g., Apple, Atari, VIC); the number of kilobytes, or units of memory (e.g., 8KB); the operating system (e.g., IBM PC-DOS 2.10, CP/M 2.2); and the form of the program (e.g., cartridge, cassette, or disk). Separate these items with commas and conclude the entry with a period.

Kilgus, Robert G. Color Scripsit. Computer software. Tandy,

1981. TRS-80, cartridge.

Pattis, Richard E. Karel the Robot: A Gentle Introduction to

the Art of Programming. Computer software.

Cybertronics, 1981.

Starks, Sparky. Diskey. Computer software. Adventure, 1982.

Atari 400/800, 32KB, disk.

Wordstar. Release 3.3. Computer software. Micropro, 1983.

4.8.2.   Material from a computer service

Treat material obtained from a computer service—such as BRS, Dialog, or Mead—like other printed material, but add a reference to the service at the end of the entry. Give the publication information as provided by the service, the name of the vendor providing the service, and the accession or identifying numbers within the service.

Schomer, Howard.   "South Africa: Beyond Fair Employment."

Harvard Business Review May-June 1983: 145+. Dialog file

122, item 119425 833160.

"Turner, Barbara Bush." American Men and Women of Science.

15th ed. Bowker, 1983. Dialog file 236, item 0107406.

```
File122:Harvard Business Review - 1971-84,Jan/Feb
(Copr. Harvard 1984)


119425          833160          **COMPLETE TEXT AVAILABLE**
South Africa: Beyond Fair Employment
Schomer, Howard - Howard Schomer Associates - United Church of Christ
HARVARD BUSINESS REVIEW, May/Jun 1983, p. 145


TEXT:
Executives  of  companies  with interests in South Africa have known for
some time that neutrality toward the government's policy of apartheid is at
least irresponsible,  if not downright dishonest.  Few actually agree with
the notion that enshrining white supremacy as a constitutional principle is
a defensible political course.
     And  so  they've  done something about it.  When the government of Prime
Minister Pieter Botha allowed limited yet independent black unions in 1979,
for  example,   some  companies  immediately  began  to  negotiate  with
representatives  of  blacks  and  bypassed  the  government-supported labor
organizations,  which are dominated by whites.  Fully 30% of the 400  U.S.
companies  with  affiliates  or subsidiaries in South Africa have committed
themselves to racial equality in their operations,  in accordance with six
principles  promulgated  in  1977  by  the Reverend Leon Sullivan, a black
social reformer who has become a  member  of  the  board  of  directors of
General Motors (for more details on the Sullivan initiative,  see the ruled
insert).
     But  are  such actions by companies enough? Absolutely not.  Events of the
last  few years cause knowledgeable corporate executives to despair whether
the white rulers of South Africa will be able to move swiftly enough toward
equal rights for all. No longer can they think that the problem will simply
go away or that the government can indefinitely contain the black drive for
equality.  The much-heralded initiative to allow independent black  unions,
taken  after  a 1976 police assault on unarmed demonstrators in Soweto that
resulted in 600 deaths, 6,000 arrests, and hundreds of banning orders,  has
been followed in 1980 to 1982 by a climate of renewed repression in which:
     More  than  a  dozen trade union leaders have been held for long periods
without trial for questioning.
     Ten prisoners have reportedly committed suicide while being held without
charge or trial under the stringent security laws,
     An unprecedented court inquiry into the  mysterious  death  of  a  white
prisoner,  Dr.  Neil Aggett,  while formally exonerating prison officials,
pointed up the kinds of torture the government uses as standard practice.
     Black political groups,  like the African National Congress,  have  been
systematically banned,   and white workers for black unions,  like Barbara
Anne Hogan, have been sentenced to ten years imprisonment for high treason.
```

The beginning of an article from the Harvard Business Review *as retrieved from Dialog. Entering the appropriate file number (122) yields a note on the holdings available. Having searched the entire holdings for appropriate terms, the system retrieved this article.*

4.8.3.   Material from an information service

Treat material obtained from an information service—such as ERIC (Educational Resources Information Center) or NTIS (National Technical Information Service)—like other printed material, but add a reference to the service at the end of the entry. If the material was published previously, give the full details of its original publication, followed by the name of the service and the identifying number within the service.

Phillips, June K., ed. Action for the '80s: A Political,

Professional, and Public Program for Foreign Language

Education. Skokie: Natl. Textbook, 1981. ERIC ED 197

599.

Spolsky, Bernard. Navajo Language Maintenance: Six-Year-Olds

in 1969. Navajo Reading Study Prog. Rept. 5.

Albuquerque: U of New Mexico, 1969. ERIC ED 043 004.

If the material was not previously published, treat its distribution by the information service as the mode of publication.

Streiff, Paul R. Some Criteria for Designing Evaluation of

TESOL Programs. ERIC, 1970. ED 040 385.

No place of publication is cited for materials distributed by the ERIC Document Reproduction Service (EDRS), since the location of this government-sponsored service changes.

4.8.4.   Radio and television programs

An entry for a radio or television program usually provides the title of the program, underlined, followed by the network (e.g., PBS), the local station and its city (e.g., KETC, St. Louis), and the date of broadcast. Where appropriate, the title of the episode, in quotation marks, should precede the title of the program, and the title of the series, neither underlined nor enclosed in quotation marks, should appear after the program (see sample entry for "The Joy Ride"). Use a comma between the station and the city (and after the city if a state abbreviation follows) and periods after all other items. For the inclusion of other information that may be pertinent (e.g., director, narrator, producer), see the sample entries.

Boris Godunov. By Modest Mussorgsky. With Martti Talvela.

    Cond. James Conlon. Metropolitan Opera. Texaco-

    Metropolitan Opera Radio Network. WGAU, Athens, GA. 29

    Jan. 1983.

The First Americans. Narr. Hugh Downs. Writ. and prod. Craig

    Fisher. NBC News Special. KNBC, Los Angeles. 21 Mar.

    1968.

Götterdämmerung. By Richard Wagner. Dir. Patrice Chereau.

    With Gwyneth Jones and Manfred Jung. Cond. Pierre

    Boulez. Bayreuth Festival Orch. PBS. WNET, New York.

    6 and 13 June 1983.

"The Joy Ride." Writ. Alfred Shaughnessy. Upstairs,

    Downstairs. Created by Eileen Atkins and Jean Marsh.

    Dir. Bill Bain. Prod. John Hawkesworth. Masterpiece

    Theatre. Introd. Alistair Cooke. PBS. WGBH, Boston. 6

    Feb. 1977.

If your reference is primarily to the work of a particular individual, cite that person's name before the title.

Dickens, Charles. The Life and Adventures of Nicholas

    Nickleby. Adapt. David Edgar. Dir. Trevor Nunn and John

    Caird. With Roger Rees and Emily Richard. Royal

Shakespeare Co. Mobil Showcase Network. WNEW, New York.

10-13 Jan. 1983.

Welles, Orson, dir. <u>War of the Worlds</u>. Writ. Howard Koch.

Based on H. G. Wells's <u>War of the Worlds</u>. Mercury

Theatre on the Air. CBS Radio. WCBS, New York. 30 Oct.

1938.

See 4.8.11 for interviews on radio and television programs; see also 4.8.5 for recordings and 4.8.7 for performances.

4.8.5.   Recordings

In an entry for a commercially available recording the person cited first (e.g., the composer, conductor, or performer) will depend on the desired emphasis. Include the title of the record or tape (or the titles of the works included), the artist(s), the manufacturer, the catalog number, and the year of issue (if unknown, write "n.d."). Commas follow the manufacturer and the number; periods follow other items. If you are using a tape recording, indicate the medium (e.g., Audiotape), neither underlined nor placed in quotation marks, immediately after the title (see sample entries for "Eliot" and "Wilgus"). Include physical characteristics at the end of the entry if the information is relevant or if the recording is not readily available (see sample entry for "Wilgus").

If the title of a recording of classical music is less important than the list of works recorded, omit it from the citation. In general, underline record titles, but do not underline or put in quotation marks the titles of musical compositions identified only by form, number, and key (see 2.5.2 as well as the sample entries for "Beethoven" and "Mozart"). You may wish to indicate, in addition to the year of issue, the actual date of recording (see sample entries for "Ellington" and "Holiday").

Beethoven, Ludwig van. Symphony no. 7 in A, op. 92. Cond.

Herbert von Karajan. Vienna Philharmonic Orch. London,

STS 15107, 1966.

Berlioz, Hector. <u>Symphonie fantastique</u>, op. 14. Cond. Georg
Solti. Chicago Symphony Orch. London, CS 6790, 1968.

Ellington, Duke, cond. Duke Ellington Orch. <u>First Carnegie
Hall Concert</u>. Rec. 23 Jan. 1943. Prestige, P-34004,
1977.

Falla, Manuel de. <u>Quatre pièces espagnoles</u>, Dance no. 2 from
<u>La vida breve</u>, "Danza de los vecinos" and "Danza de la
molinera" from <u>El sombrero de tres picos</u>, "Danza del
terror" from <u>El amor brujo</u>, and <u>Fantasía bética</u>. Alicia
de Larrocha, pianist. Turnabout-Vox, TVS 34742, 1978.

Holiday, Billie. "God Bless the Child." Rec. 9 May 1941.
<u>Billie Holiday: The Golden Years</u>. Columbia, C3L 21,
1962.

Joplin, Scott. <u>Treemonisha</u>. With Carmen Balthrop, Betty
Allen, and Curtis Rayam. Cond. Gunther Schuller.
Houston Grand Opera Orch. and Chorus. Deutsche
Grammophon, S-2707 083, 1975.

Lloyd Webber, Andrew. <u>Cats</u>. With Elaine Page and Brian
Blessed. Cond. David Firman. Geffen, 2GHS 2017, 1981.

Mozart, Wolfgang A. Symphony no. 35 in D and Overtures to <u>The
Marriage of Figaro</u>, <u>The Magic Flute</u>, and <u>Don Giovanni</u>.
Cond. Antonia Brico. Mostly Mozart Orch. Columbia,
M33888, 1976.

Sondheim, Stephen. <u>Sweeney Todd</u>. With Angela Lansbury and
Len Cariou. Cond. Paul Gemignani. RCA, CBL2-3379, 1979.

Verdi, Giuseppe. <u>Rigoletto</u>. With Joan Sutherland, Luciano

Pavarotti, Sherrill Milnes, and Martti Talvela. Cond.

Richard Bonynge. London Symphony Orch. and Ambrosian

Opera Chorus. London, OSA-12105, 1973.

Treat a recording of the spoken word as you would a musical record-ing. Begin with the speaker, the writer, or the production director, the choice depending on the desired emphasis.

Eliot, T. S. Old Possum's Book of Practical Cats. Audiotape.

Read by John Gielgud and Irene Worth. Caedmon, CP 1713,

1983.

Frost, Robert. "The Road Not Taken." Robert Frost Reads His

Poetry. Caedmon, TC 1060, 1956.

Lehmann, Lotte. Lotte Lehmann Reading German Poetry.

Caedmon, TC 1072, 1958.

Murrow, Edward R. Year of Decision: 1943. Columbia, CPS-

3872, 1957.

Shakespeare, William. Othello. Dir. John Dexter. With

Laurence Olivier, Maggie Smith, Frank Finley, and Derek

Jacobi. RCA, VDM-100, 1964.

Welles, Orson, dir. War of the Worlds. Writ. Howard Koch.

Based on H. G. Wells's War of the Worlds. Mercury

Theatre on the Air. Rec. 30 Oct. 1938. Evolution, 4001,

1969.

Do not underline or enclose in quotation marks the title of a private or archival recording or tape. Include the date recorded (if known), the location and identifying number of the recording, and the physical charac-teristics (if ascertainable).

Wilgus, D. K. Southern Folk Tales. Audiotape. Rec. 23-25

    Mar. 1965. U of California, Los Angeles, Archives of

    Folklore. B.76.82. 7 1/2 ips, 7" reel.

   In citing the jacket notes, libretto, or other material accompanying a
recording, give the author's name, the title of the material (if any), and
a description of the material (e.g., Jacket notes, Libretto). Then provide
the usual bibliographic information for a recording.

Colette. Libretto. L'enfant et les sortilèges. Music by

    Maurice Ravel. With Suzanne Danco and Hugues Cuenod.

    Cond. Ernest Ansermet. Orch. de la Suisse Romande.

    Richmond-London, SR 33086, n.d.

Collins, Judy. Jacket notes. Antonia Brico, cond. Mostly

    Mozart Orch. Symphony no. 35 in D and Overtures to The

    Marriage of Figaro, The Magic Flute, and Don Giovanni.

    By Wolfgang A. Mozart. Columbia, M33888, 1976.

Lawrence, Vera Brodsky. "Scott Joplin and Treemonisha."

    Libretto. Treemonisha. By Scott Joplin. Deutsche

    Grammophon, S-2707 083, 1975. 10-12.

Lewiston, David. Jacket notes. The Balinese Gamelan: Music

    from the Morning of the World. Nonesuch Explorer Series,

    H-2015, n.d.

4.8.6. Films, filmstrips, slide programs, and videotapes

   A film citation usually begins with the title, underlined, and includes
the director, the distributor, and the year. You may include other data

that seem pertinent: the names of contributors, such as the writer, performers, and producer, would follow the title; physical characteristics, such as the size and length of the film, would go after the date.

A bout de souffle [Breathless]. Dir. Jean-Luc Godard. With

    Jean-Paul Belmondo and Jean Seberg. Beauregard, 1960.

Det Sjunde Inseglet [The Seventh Seal]. Dir. Ingmar Bergman.

    Svensk Filmindustri, 1956.

If you are citing the contribution of a particular individual, begin with that person's name.

Chaplin, Charles, dir. Modern Times. With Chaplin and

    Paulette Goddard. United Artists, 1936.

Lerner, Alan Jay, screenwriter. An American in Paris. Dir.

    Vincente Minnelli. Prod. Arthur Freed. Music by George

    Gershwin. Lyrics by Ira Gershwin. With Gene Kelly,

    Leslie Caron, and Oscar Levant. MGM, 1951.

Mifune, Toshiro, actor. Rashomon. Dir. Akira Kurosawa. With

    Machiko Kyo. Daiei, 1950.

Rota, Nino, composer. Giulietta degli spiriti [Juliet of the

    Spirits]. Dir. Federico Fellini. With Giulietta Masina.

    Rizzoli, 1965.

In citing a filmstrip, slide program, or videotape, include the medium, neither underlined nor enclosed in quotation marks, immediately after the title and then give the usual bibliographic information for films.

Alcohol Use and Its Medical Consequences: A Comprehensive

    Teaching Program for Biomedical Education. Slide

program. Developed by Project Cork, Dartmouth Medical

School. Milner-Fenwick, 1982. 46 slides.

Consumer Awareness: Supply, Demand, Competition, and Prices.

Sound filmstrip. Prod. Visual Education. Maclean Hunter

Learning Resources, 1981. 85 fr., 11 min.

Creation vs. Evolution: "Battle of the Classroom."

Videocassette. Dir. Ryall Wilson. PBS Video, 1982. 58

min.

4.8.7. Performances

An entry for a performance (e.g., a stage play, opera, ballet, or concert) usually begins with the title, contains information similar to that for a film (see 4.8.6), and concludes with the theater, a comma, the city (followed where necessary by a comma and a state abbreviation), a period, and the date of the performance.

Boris Godunov. By Modest Mussorgsky. Dir. August Everding.

Cond. James Conlon. With Martti Talvela. Metropolitan

Opera. Metropolitan Opera House, New York. 29 Jan.

1983.

Cats. By Andrew Lloyd Webber. Based on T. S. Eliot's Old

Possum's Book of Practical Cats. Dir. Trevor Nunn. New

London Theatre, London. 11 May 1981.

La Fanciulla del West. By Giacomo Puccini. Dir. Patrick

Bakman. Cond. Stefan Minde. With Marilyn Zschau and

Vladimir Popov. Portland Opera Assn. Civic Auditorium,

Portland, OR. 17 Mar. 1983.

Hamlet. By William Shakespeare. Dir. John Gielgud. With

Richard Burton. Shubert Theatre, Boston. 4 Mar. 1964.

If you are citing the contribution of a particular individual, begin with that person's name.

Balanchine, George, chor. <u>Mozartiana</u>. With Suzanne Farrell.

New York City Ballet. New York State Theater, New York.

20 Nov. 1981.

Caldwell, Sarah, dir. and cond. <u>La Traviata</u>. By Giuseppe

Verdi. With Beverly Sills. Opera Co. of Boston.

Orpheum Theatre, Boston. 4 Nov. 1972.

Ellington, Duke, cond. Duke Ellington Orch. Concert.

Carnegie Hall, New York. 23 Jan. 1943.

Joplin, Scott. <u>Treemonisha</u>. Dir. Frank Corsaro. Cond.

Gunther Schuller. With Carmen Balthrop, Betty Allen, and

Curtis Rayam. Houston Grand Opera. Miller Theatre,

Houston. 18 May 1975.

Prince, Harold, dir. <u>Sweeney Todd</u>. By Stephen Sondheim.

With Angela Lansbury and Len Cariou. Uris Theatre, New

York. 1 Mar. 1979.

Shaw, Robert, cond. Atlanta Symphony Orch. Concert. Atlanta

Arts Center, Atlanta. 14 Dec. 1981.

For broadcasts and telecasts of performances, see 4.8.4; for recordings of performances, see 4.8.5.

4.8.8.   Musical compositions

In citing a musical composition, begin with the composer's name. Underline the title of an opera, a ballet, or instrumental music identified by name (e.g., *Symphonie fantastique*), but do not underline or put in quotation marks an instrumental composition identified only by form, number, and key.

Beethoven, Ludwig van. Symphony no. 7 in A, op. 92.

Berlioz, Hector. <u>Symphonie fantastique</u>, op. 14.

Wagner, Richard. <u>Götterdämmerung</u>.

Treat a published score, however, like a book. Give the title as it appears on the title page and underline it.

Beethoven, Ludwig van. <u>Symphony No. 7 in A, Op. 92</u>. Kalmus

   Miniature Orch. Scores 7. New York: Kalmus, n.d.

For recordings of musical compositions, see 4.8.5; see also 4.8.4 for radio and television programs and 4.8.7 for performances.

4.8.9.   Works of art

In citing a work of art, state the artist's name first. In general, underline the title of a painting or sculpture. Name the institution housing the work (e.g., a museum), followed by a comma and the city.

Bernini, Gianlorenzo. <u>Ecstasy of St. Teresa</u>. Santa Maria

   della Vittoria, Rome.

Rembrandt van Rijn. <u>Aristotle Contemplating the Bust of</u>

   <u>Homer</u>. Metropolitan Museum of Art, New York.

If you use a photograph of the work, indicate not only the institution and the city but also the complete publication information for the work in which the photograph appears.

Cassatt, Mary. <u>Mother and Child</u>. Wichita Art Museum,

   Wichita. Slide 22 of <u>American Painting: 1560-1913</u>. By

   John Pearce. New York: McGraw, 1964.

Houdon, Jean-Antoine. <u>Statue of Voltaire</u>. Comédie Française,

Paris. Illus. 51 in <u>Literature through Art: A New</u>

<u>Approach to French Literature</u>. By Helmut A. Hatzfeld.

New York: Oxford UP, 1952.

4.8.10. Letters

As bibliographic entries, letters fall into three general categories: (1) published letters, (2) letters in archives, and (3) letters received by the researcher. Treat a published letter like a work in a collection (see 4.5.8), adding the date of the letter and the number (if the editor has assigned one).

Thackeray, William Makepeace. "To George Henry Lewes." 6

Mar. 1848. Letter 452 in <u>Letters and Private Papers of</u>

<u>William Makepeace Thackeray</u>. Ed. Gordon N. Ray. Vol. 2.

Cambridge: Harvard UP, 1945. 353-54. 4 vols. 1945-46.

If you are citing more than one letter from a published collection, however, provide a single entry for the entire work and give individual citations in the text (see 4.5.10).

In citing unpublished letters, follow the basic guidelines for manuscripts and typescripts (see 4.8.15) and for private and archival recordings and tapes (see 4.8.5).

Benton, Thomas Hart. Letter to Charles Fremont. 22 June

1847. John Charles Fremont Papers. Southwest Museum

Library, Los Angeles.

Cite a letter personally received as follows:

Copland, Aaron. Letter to the author. 17 May 1982.

4.8.11. Interviews

Interviews fall into a number of categories: (1) published or recorded interviews, (2) interviews on radio or television, and (3) interviews conducted by the researcher. Begin with the name of the person interviewed. If the interview is part of a publication, recording, or program, put the title, if any, in quotation marks; if the interview is the entire work, underline the title. If the interview is untitled, use the descriptive label "Interview," neither underlined nor enclosed in quotation marks. (Interviewers' names may be included if known and if pertinent; see sample entry below for "Stravinsky.") Conclude with the usual bibliographic information required for the entry.

Fellini, Federico. "The Long Interview." Juliet of the

Spirits. Ed. Tullio Kezich. Trans. Howard Greenfield.

New York: Ballantine, 1966. 17-64.

Gordon, Suzanne. Interview. All Things Considered. Natl.

Public Radio. WNYC, New York. 1 June 1983.

Kundera, Milan. Interview. New York Times 18 Jan. 1982, late

ed., sec. 3: 13+.

Stravinsky, Igor. Conversation with Igor Stravinsky. With

Robert Craft. Berkeley: U of California P, 1980.

Wolfe, Tom. Interview. The Wrong Stuff: American

Architecture. Videocassette. Dir. Tom Bettag. Carousel

Films, 1983.

In citing a personally conducted interview, give the name of the interviewee, the kind of interview (Personal interview, Telephone interview), and the date.

Pei, I. M. Personal interview. 27 July 1983.

Poussaint, Alvin F. Telephone interview. 10 Dec. 1980.

4.8.12. Maps and charts

In general, treat maps and charts like anonymous books, but add the appropriate descriptive label (e.g., Map, Chart).

Canada. Map. Chicago: Rand, 1983.

Grammar and Punctuation. Chart. Grand Haven: School Zone,

   1980.

For guidance in citing such sources as dioramas, flashcards, games, globes, kits, and models, see Eugene B. Fleischer, *A Style Manual for Citing Microform and Nonprint Media* (Chicago: Amer. Library Assn., 1978).

4.8.13. Cartoons

To cite a cartoon, state the cartoonist's name, the title of the cartoon (if any) in quotation marks, and the descriptive label "Cartoon," neither underlined nor enclosed in quotation marks. Conclude with the usual publication information.

Addams, Charles. Cartoon. New Yorker 21 Feb. 1983: 41.

Schulz, Charles. "Peanuts." Cartoon. Star-Ledger [Newark,

   NJ] 4 Sept. 1980: 72.

4.8.14. Lectures, speeches, and addresses

Give the speaker's name, the title of the lecture (if known) in quotation marks, the meeting and the sponsoring organization (if applicable), the location, and the date. If there is no title, use an appropriate descriptive label (e.g., Lecture, Address, Keynote speech), neither underlined nor enclosed in quotation marks.

Ciardi, John. Address. Opening General Sess. NCTE

   Convention. Washington, 19 Nov. 1982.

Ridley, Florence. "Forget the Past, Reject the Future: Chaos

   Is Come Again." Div. on Teaching of Literature, MLA

   Convention. Los Angeles, 28 Dec. 1982.

4.8.15   Manuscripts and typescripts

In citing a manuscript or a typescript, state the author, the title (e.g., *La chanson de Roland*) or a description of the material (e.g., Notebook), the form of the material (ms. for manuscript, ts. for typescript), and any identifying number assigned to it. If a library or other research institution houses the material, give its name and location.

La chanson de Roland. Digby ms. 23. Bodleian Library,

   Oxford.

Smith, John. "Shakespeare's Dark Lady." Unpublished essay,

   1983.

Twain, Mark. Notebook 32, ts. Mark Twain Papers. U of

   California, Berkeley.

4.8.16.   Legal references

The citation of legal documents and law cases may be complicated. If your paper requires many such references, consult the most recent edition of *A Uniform System of Citation* (Cambridge: Harvard Law Rev. Assn.), an indispensable guide in this field.

In general, do not underline or enclose in quotation marks laws, acts, and similar documents in either the text or the list of works cited (e.g., Declaration of Independence, Constitution of the United States, Taft-Hartley Act). Such works are usually cited by sections, with the year number added if relevant. Although lawyers and legal scholars adopt many abbreviations in their citations, use only familiar abbreviations when writing for a more general audience.

15 US Code.   Sec. 78j(b).   1964.

U. S. Const.   Art. 1, sec. 1

Note that in references to the United States Code, often abbreviated as USC, the title number precedes the code: 12 USC, 15 USC, etc. Alphabetize under "United States Code" even if you use the abbreviation. When including more than one reference to the code, list individual entries in numerical order.

Names of law cases are both abbreviated and shortened (Brown v. Board of Ed. *for* Oliver Brown versus Board of Education of Topeka, Kansas), but the first important word of each party is always spelled out. Unlike laws, names of cases are underlined in the text but not in bibliographic entries. In citing a case, include, in addition to the names of the first plaintiff and the first defendant, the volume, name (not underlined), and page (in that order) of the law report cited; the name of the court that decided the case; and the year in which it was decided. Once again, considerable abbreviation is the norm. The following citation, for example, refers to page 755 of volume 148 of the *United States Patent Quarterly* dealing with the case of Stevens against the National Broadcasting Company, which was decided by the California Superior Court in 1966.

Stevens v. National Broadcasting Co.   148 USPQ 755.   Calif.

  Super. Ct.   1966.

5 DOCUMENTING SOURCES

5.1. What to document

In scholarly writing, everything derived from an outside source requires documentation — not only direct quotations and paraphrases but also information and ideas. Of course, good judgment as well as ethics should guide you in interpreting this rule. Although you rarely need, for example, to give sources for familiar proverbs ("You can't judge a book by its cover"), well-known quotations ("We shall overcome"), or common knowledge ("George Washington was the first president of the United States"), you must indicate the origin of any appropriated material that readers might otherwise mistake for your own. (On plagiarism, see 1.4.)

5.2. Parenthetical documentation and the list of works cited

The list of works cited at the end of your manuscript plays an important role in your acknowledgment of sources (see ch. 4), but it does not in itself provide sufficiently detailed and precise documentation. You must specify what you have derived from each source and where in that work you found the material. The most practical way to supply this information is to insert brief parenthetical acknowledgments in the manuscript wherever you incorporate another's words, facts, or ideas. Usually, the author's last name and a page reference are all that you need.

Ancient writers attributed the invention of the monochord to

Pythagoras in the sixth century BC (Marcuse 197).

The parenthetical reference indicates that the information on the monochord comes from page 197 of the book by Marcuse included in the alphabetically arranged list of works cited that follows the text. Thus, it enables the reader to find complete publication information for the source:

```
Marcuse, Sibyl. A Survey of Musical Instruments. New York:

   Harper, 1975.
```

The sample references in 5.5 offer recommendations for documenting many other kinds of sources.

5.3. Information required in parenthetical documentation

In determining the information needed to document sources accurately, keep the following guidelines in mind:

1. References in the text must clearly point to specific sources in the list of works cited. The information in the parenthetical reference, therefore, must match the corresponding information in the list. When the list contains only one work by the cited author (or editor, translator, speaker, creative artist, etc.—whichever name you have chosen to begin the entry in the list of works cited), you need give only the author's last name to identify the work (though you would, of course, have to give the first name as well if two authors on the list had the same last name). If the work has more than one author, give all the last names or one last name followed by "et al.," in keeping with the bibliographic entry (see 5.5.1). If the work is listed by a corporate author, use that name, or a shortened version of it (see 5.5.5); if the work is listed by title, use the title, or a shortened version (see 5.5.4); if the list contains more than one work by the author, give the title cited, or a shortened version, after the author's last name (see 5.5.6).

2. Identify the location of the borrowed information as specifically as possible. Give the relevant page number(s) (see 5.5.2) or, if citing a multivolume work, the volume and page number(s) (see 5.5.3). In references to literary works, it may be appropriate to give information other than, or in addition to, the page numbers—for example, the chapter, the book, the stanza, or the act, scene, and line (see 5.5.8). You may omit page numbers when citing one-page articles, articles arranged alphabetically in works like encyclopedias, and, of course, nonprint sources (see 5.5.4).

5.4. Readability

Keep parenthetical references as brief — and as few — as clarity and accuracy permit. Give only the information needed to identify a source,
and do not add a parenthetical reference unnecessarily. If you are citing
an entire work, for example, rather than a specific part of it, the author's
name in the text may be the only documentation required. The statement "Booth has devoted an entire book to the subject" needs no parenthetical documentation if the list of works cited includes only one work
by Booth. If, for the reader's convenience, you wished to name the book
in your text, you could recast the sentence: "In *The Rhetoric of Fiction* Booth
deals with this subject exclusively." Remember that there is a direct relation between what you integrate into your text and what you place in
parentheses. If, for example, you include an author's name in a sentence,
you need not repeat it in the parenthetical page citation that follows. It
will be clear that the reference is to the work of the author you have mentioned. The paired sentences below illustrate how to cite authors in the
text to keep parenthetical references concise.

Author's name in text

Frye has argued this point before (178-85).

Author's name in reference

This point has been argued before (Frye 178-85).

Authors' names in text

Others, like Wellek and Warren (310-15), hold an opposite
point of view.

Authors' names in reference

Others hold an opposite point of view (e.g., Wellek and Warren
310-15).

Author's name in text

Only Daiches has seen this relation (2: 776-77).

Author's name in reference

Only one critic has seen this relation (Daiches 2: 776-77).

Author's name in text

It may be true, as Robertson writes, that "in the appreciation of medieval art the attitude of the observer is of primary importance . . ." (136).

Author's name in reference

It may be true that "in the appreciation of medieval art the attitude of the observer is of primary importance . . ." (Robertson 136).

To avoid interrupting the flow of your writing, place the parenthetical reference where a pause would naturally occur (preferably at the end of a sentence), as near as possible to the material it documents. The parenthetical reference precedes the punctuation mark that concludes the sentence, clause, or phrase containing the borrowed material.

In his <u>Autobiography</u>, Benjamin Franklin states that he prepared a list of thirteen virtues (135-37).

If a quotation comes at the end of the sentence, clause, or phrase, insert the parenthetical reference between the closing quotation mark and the concluding punctuation mark.

Ernst Rose writes, "The highly spiritual view of the world

presented in <u>Siddartha</u> exercised its appeal on West and East

alike" (74).

If the quotation, whether of poetry or prose, is set off from the text (see 2.6.2–3), skip two spaces after the concluding punctuation mark of the quotation and insert the parenthetical reference.

John K. Mahon offers this comment on the War of 1812:

> Financing the war was very difficult at the time.
>
> Baring Brothers, a banking firm of the enemy
>
> country, handled routine accounts for the United
>
> States overseas, but the firm would take on no
>
> loans.   The loans were in the end absorbed by
>
> wealthy Americans at great hazard--also, as it
>
> turned out, at great profit to them. (385)

If you need to document several sources for a statement, you may cite them in a note to avoid unduly disrupting the text (see 5.6).

See chapter 7 for a discussion of the special considerations for dissertations.

5.5.   Sample references

Each of the following sections concludes with a list of the works it cites. Note that the lists for the first five sections (5.5.1 to 5.5.5) do not include more than one work by the same author. On citing two or more works by an author, see 5.5.6.

5.5.1.   Citing an entire work

If you are citing an entire work, not just a part, it is usually better to include the author's name in the text than in a parenthetical reference.

But Judith Kauffman has offered another view.

The Seller anthology <u>Ethnic Theater in the United States</u> includes many examples of this influence.

Kurosawa's <u>Rashomon</u> was one of the first Japanese films to attract a Western audience.

John Ciardi's remarks drew warm applause.

I vividly recall the Caldwell production of <u>La Traviata</u>.

Pattis's introduction to computer programming has received widespread praise.

Gilbert and Gubar published a pathbreaking effort on the subject.

Edens et al. have a useful collection of essays on teaching Shakespeare.

If, however, you choose not to use the author's name in the text, include it in a parenthetical reference. When citing an entire work, you usually need only the last name of the author. If two or three names begin the entry, give the last name of each person listed. If one name followed by "et al." begins the entry, give the last name of the person listed, followed by "et al.," without any intervening punctuation: Edens et al. Omit other abbreviations, such as ed., trans., comp.: There is only one comprehensive anthology in this field (Seller). (See 5.5.4 for works listed by title.)

Works Cited

Caldwell, Sarah, dir. and cond. <u>La Traviata</u>. By Giuseppe

Verdi. With Beverly Sills. Opera Co. of Boston.

Orpheum Theatre, Boston. 4 Nov. 1972.

Ciardi, John. Address. Opening General Sess. NCTE

Convention, Washington. 19 Nov. 1982.

Edens, Walter, et al., eds. <u>Teaching Shakespeare</u>. Princeton:

Princeton UP, 1977.

Gilbert, Sandra M., and Susan Gubar. <u>The Madwoman in the</u>

<u>Attic: The Woman Writer and the Nineteenth-Century</u>

<u>Literary Imagination</u>. New Haven: Yale UP, 1979.

Kauffman, Judith. "Musique et matière romanesque dans

<u>Moderato cantabile</u> de Marguerite Duras." <u>Etudes</u>

<u>littéraires</u> 15 (1982): 97-112.

Kurosawa, Akira, dir. <u>Rashomon</u>. With Toshiro Mifune and

Michiko Kyo. Daiei, 1950.

Pattis, Richard E. <u>Karel the Robot: A Gentle Introduction to</u>

<u>the Art of Programming</u>. Computer software.

Cybertronics, 1981.

Seller, Maxine Schwartz, ed. <u>Ethnic Theater in the United</u>

<u>States</u>. Westport: Greenwood, 1983.

5.5.2. Citing part of an article or of a single-volume book

If you quote, paraphrase, or otherwise use a specific passage in a book or article, give the relevant page numbers. If the author's name is in the text, only the page reference need appear in parentheses. If the context does not clearly identify the author, add the author's last name before the page reference. Leave a space between them, but do not insert punctuation or write "page(s)" or the abbreviation "p." or "pp."

Kenneth Clark has raised some interesting questions concerning artistic "masterpieces" (1-5, 12-13).

Another particularly appealing passage is the opening of García Márquez's story "A Very Old Man with Enormous Wings" (105).

Among intentional spoonerisms, the "punlike metathesis of distinctive features may serve to weld together words etymologically unrelated but close in their sound and meaning" (Jakobson and Waugh 304).

In Hansberry's A Raisin in the Sun the rejection of Lindner's tempting offer permits Walter's family to pursue the new life they had long dreamed about (274-75).

As Katharina M. Wilson has written, "Intended or not, the echoes of Tertullian's exhortations in the Utopia provide yet another level of ambiguity to More's ironic commentary on social and moral conditions both in sixteenth-century Europe and in Nowhere-Land" (73).

A 1983 report found "a decline in the academic quality of students choosing teaching as a career" (Hook 10).

Works Cited

Clark, Kenneth. What Is a Masterpiece? London: Thames, 1979.

García Márquez, Gabriel. "A Very Old Man with Enormous

Wings." "Leaf Storm" and Other Stories. Trans. Gregory

Rabassa. New York: Harper, 1972. 105-12.

Hansberry, Lorraine. A Raisin in the Sun. Black Theater: A

Twentieth-Century Collection of the Work of Its Best

Playwrights. Ed. Lindsay Patterson. New York: Dodd,

1971. 221-76.

Hook, Janet. "Raise Standards of Admission, Colleges Urged."

Chronicle of Higher Education 4 May 1983: 1+.

Jakobson, Roman, and Linda R. Waugh. The Sound Shape of

Language. Bloomington: Indiana UP, 1979.

Wilson, Katharina M. "Tertullian's De cultu foeminarum and

Utopia." Moreana 73 (1982): 69-74.

5.5.3.   Citing volume and page numbers of a multivolume work

To cite volume numbers as well as page numbers of a multivolume work, give the volume number, a colon, a space, and the page reference: (Wellek 2: 1-10). Use neither the words "volume" and "page" nor abbreviations. It is understood that the number *before* the colon identifies the volume and the number(s) *after* the colon the page(s). If, however, you wish to refer parenthetically to an entire volume of a multivolume work, so that there is no need to cite pages, place a comma after the author's name and write "vol." before the number: (Wellek, vol. 2). If you integrate such a reference into a sentence, spell out "volume" instead of abbreviating it: In volume 2, Wellek deals with. . . .

Interest in Afro-American literature in the 1960s and 1970s

inevitably led to "a significant reassessment of the aesthetic

and humanistic achievements of black writers" (Inge, Duke, and
Bryer 1: v).

Between the years 1945 and 1972, the political party system in
the United States underwent profound changes (Schlesinger,
vol. 4).

Daiches is useful on the Restoration (2: 538-89), as he is on
other periods.

Works Cited

Daiches, David. A Critical History of English Literature.

2nd ed. 2 vols. New York: Ronald, 1970.

Inge, M. Thomas, Maurice Duke, and Jackson R. Bryer, eds.

Black American Writers: Bibliographical Essays. 2 vols.

New York: St. Martin's, 1978.

Schlesinger, Arthur M., gen. ed. History of U.S. Political

Parties. 4 vols. New York: Chelsea, 1973.

5.5.4. Citing a work listed by title

In a parenthetical reference to a work alphabetized by title in the list
of works cited, the title (if brief), or a shortened version, replaces the
author's name before the page number(s). Omit a page reference, however, if you are citing a work with alphabetized entries (such as a dictionary or an encyclopedia), a one-page article, or, of course, a nonprint source.
When condensing the title of an anonymous work, begin with the word
by which it is alphabetized in the list of works cited. It would be a mistake, for example, to cite the book Glossary of Terms Used in Heraldry as Her-

aldry since your reader would then look for the bibliographic entry under "h" rather than "g." (See also 5.5.5, on citing books by corporate authors.)

The nine grades of mandarins were "distinguished by the color of the button on the hats of office . . ." ("Mandarin").

According to the Handbook of Korea, much Korean sculpture is associated with Buddhism (241-47).

Computerworld has devoted a thoughtful editorial to the issue of government and technology ("Uneasy Silence"), and one hopes that such public discussion will continue in the future.

Later, when the characters are confronted by tragedy, they take on greater depth ("Joy Ride").

Works Cited

A Handbook of Korea. 4th ed. Seoul: Korean Overseas
   Information Service, Ministry of Culture and Information,
   1982.
"The Joy Ride." Writ. Alfred Shaughnessy. Upstairs,
   Downstairs. Created by Eileen Atkins and Jean Marsh.
   Dir. Bill Bain. Prod. John Hawkesworth. Masterpiece
   Theatre. Introd. Alistair Cooke. PBS. WGBH, Boston.
   6 Feb. 1977.
"Mandarin." Encyclopedia Americana. 1980 ed.
"An Uneasy Silence." Editorial. Computerworld 28 Mar. 1983:
   54.

5.5.5.   Citing a work by a corporate author

To cite a work listed by a corporate author, you may use the corporate author's name followed by a page reference: (United Nations, Economic Commission for Africa 79–86). It is better, however, to include such a long name in the text to avoid interrupting the reading with an extended parenthetical reference.

In 1963 the United Nations' Economic Commission for Africa

predicted that Africa would evolve into an industrially

advanced economy within fifty years (1, 4-6).

The Commission on the Humanities has concluded that "the

humanities are inescapably bound to literacy" (69).

Works Cited

Commission on the Humanities. The Humanities in American

    Life: Report of the Commission on the Humanities.

    Berkeley: U of California P, 1980.

United Nations. Economic Commission for Africa. Industrial

    Growth in Africa. New York: United Nations, 1963.

5.5.6.   Citing two or more works by the same author(s)

To cite one of two or more works by the same author(s), put a comma after the last name(s) of the author(s) and add the title of the work (if brief) or a shortened version and the relevant page reference: (Borroff, *Wallace Stevens* 2), (Durant and Durant, *Age of Voltaire* 214–48). If you state the author's name in the text, give only the title and page reference: (*Wallace Stevens* 2), (*Age of Voltaire* 214–48). If you include both the author's name and the title in the text, indicate only the pertinent page number(s) in parentheses: (2), (214–48).

Borroff finds Stevens "dominated by two powerful and

contending temperamental strains" (<u>Wallace Stevens</u> 2).

In <u>The Age of Voltaire</u> the Durants portray eighteenth-century

England as "a humble satellite" in the world of music and art

(214-48).

As E. L. Doctorow has written, "The Dreiserian universe is

composed of merchants, workers, club-men, managers, actors,

salesmen, doormen, cops, derelicts--a Balzacian population

unified by the rules of commerce and the ideals of property

and social position" (Introduction ix).

The <u>Gawain</u> poet has been called a "master of juxtaposition"

(Borroff, <u>Sir Gawain</u> viii) and has been praised for other

poetic achievements.

To Will and Ariel Durant, creative men and women make "history

forgivable by enriching our heritage and our lives" (<u>Dual</u>

<u>Autobiography</u> 406).

The brief but dramatic conclusion of chapter 13 of Doctorow's

<u>Welcome to Hard Times</u> constitutes the climax of the novel

(209-12).

Works Cited

Borroff, Marie, trans. Sir Gawain and the Green Knight. New

York: Norton, 1967.

---, ed. Wallace Stevens: A Collection of Critical Essays.

Englewood Cliffs: Prentice, 1963.

Doctorow, E. L. Introduction. Sister Carrie. By Theodore

Dreiser. New York: Bantam, 1982. v-xi.

---. Welcome to Hard Times. 1960. New York: Bantam, 1976.

Durant, Will, and Ariel Durant. The Age of Voltaire. New

York: Simon, 1965. Vol. 9 of The Story of Civilization.

11 vols. 1935-75.

---. A Dual Autobiography. New York: Simon, 1977.

5.5.7. Citing indirect sources

Whenever possible, take material from the original source, not a second-hand one. Sometimes, however, only an indirect source is available: for example, someone's published account of another's spoken remarks. If you quote or paraphrase a quotation from another book, write "qtd. in" ("quoted in") before the indirect source you cite in your parenthetical reference. (You may document the original source in a note; see 5.6.1.)

Samuel Johnson admitted that Edmund Burke was an

"extraordinary man" (qtd. in Boswell 2: 450).

The remarks of Bernardo Segni and Lionardo Salviati

demonstrate that they were not faithful disciples of Aristotle

(qtd. in Weinberg 1: 405, 616-17).

Works Cited

Boswell, James. The Life of Johnson. Ed. George Birkbeck

Hill and L. F. Powell. 6 vols. Oxford: Clarendon,

1934-50.

Weinberg, Bernard. A History of Literary Criticism in the

Italian Renaissance. 2 vols. Chicago: U of Chicago P,

1961.

5.5.8.   Citing literary works

In references to classic prose works available in several editions (e.g., novels and plays), it is helpful to provide more information than just the page number of the edition used; a chapter number, for example, would enable readers to locate a quotation in any copy of the novel. In such references, give the page number first, add a semicolon, and then give other identifying information, using appropriate abbreviations — for example, (130; ch. 9), (271; bk. 4, ch. 2).

When we first encounter Raskolnikov in Crime and Punishment,

Dostoevsky presents us with a man contemplating a terrible act

but terrified of meeting his talkative landlady on the stairs

(1; pt. 1, ch. 1).

Mary Wollstonecraft recollects in A Vindication of the Rights

of Woman many "women who, not led by degrees to proper

studies, and not permitted to choose for themselves, have

indeed been overgrown children . . ." (185; ch. 13, sec. 2).

In one version of the story, William Tell's son urges his

reluctant father to shoot the arrow (Sastre 315; sc. 6).

In citing classic verse plays and poems, omit page numbers and cite by division(s) (e.g., canto, book, part, act, or scene) and line(s), with periods separating the various numbers—for example, *Iliad* 9.19 refers to book 9, line 19, of Homer's *Iliad*. Never use the abbreviations "l." or "ll.," which can be confused with numerals, in references to poetic works. Instead, if it is not immediately obvious that you are citing only line numbers, initially write "line" or "lines"; once you have established that the numbers designate lines, use the numbers alone.

In general, use arabic numerals rather than roman numerals in citing division and page numbers. But always use roman numerals, of course, when citing pages that are so numbered (e.g., a preface). In addition, some prefer roman numerals for citing acts and scenes in plays (e.g., *King Lear* IV.i). On numbers, see 2.7.

When included in parenthetical references, the titles of the books of the Bible and of famous literary works are often abbreviated—for example, 1 Chron. 21.8, Rev. 21.3, *Oth.* 4.2.7–13, *FQ* 3.3.53.3. (For a selected list of accepted abbreviations for literary and religious works, see 6.6.) Follow prevailing practices for other abbreviations (*Troilus* for Chaucer's *Troilus and Criseyde*, *DQ* for Cervantes's *Don Quixote*, *PL* for Milton's *Paradise Lost*, "Nightingale" for Keats's "Ode to a Nightingale," etc.). In the following example the reference is to lines 1791 and 1792 of book 5 of Chaucer's *Troilus and Criseyde*.

Using a figure much imitated by later English poets, Chaucer

urges one of his "litel boks" to kiss "the steppes, where as

thow seest pace / Virgile, Ovide, Omer, Lucan, and Stace"

(<u>Troilus</u> 5.1791-92).

Works Cited

Chaucer, Geoffrey. <u>The Works of Geoffrey Chaucer</u>. Ed. F. N.

Robinson. 2nd ed. Boston: Houghton, 1957.

Dostoevsky, Feodor. <u>Crime and Punishment</u>. Trans. Jessie

Coulson. Ed. George Gibian. New York: Norton, 1964.

Sastre, Alfonso. <u>Sad Are the Eyes of William Tell</u>. Trans.

Leonard Pronko. <u>The New Wave Spanish Drama</u>. Ed. George

Wellwarth. New York: New York UP, 1970. 165-321.

Wollstonecraft, Mary. A Vindication of the Rights of Woman.

    Ed. Carol H. Poston. New York: Norton, 1975.

5.5.9. Citing more than one work in a single parenthetical reference

If you wish to include two or more works in a single parenthetical reference, cite each work as you normally would in a reference, but use semicolons to separate the citations.

(Frye 42; Brée 101-33)

(National Committee 25-35; Brody C5)

(Potter et al., vol. 1; Boyle 96-125)

(Wellek and Warren; Booth, Critical Understanding 45-52)

(Blocker, Plummer, and Richardson 52-57; Carnegie Council 15)

(Booth, "Kenneth Burke's" 22; Cassirer 1: 295-319)

Keep in mind, however, that long parenthetical references — for example, (Stratman; Potter et al. 1: 176-202; Bondanella and Bondanella, "Lauda"; Curley ii-vii; Rey-Flaud 37-43, 187-201) — may prove intrusive and disconcerting to the reader. To avoid an excessive disruption, cite multiple sources in a note rather than in parentheses in the text (see 5.6.2).

Works Cited

Blocker, Clyde E., Robert H. Plummer, and Richard C.

    Richardson, Jr. The Two-Year College: A Social

    Synthesis. Englewood Cliffs: Prentice, 1965.

Bondanella, Peter, and Julia Conaway Bondanella, eds.

Dictionary of Italian Literature. Westport: Greenwood, 1979.

Booth, Wayne C. *Critical Understanding: The Powers and Limits of Pluralism*. Chicago: U of Chicago P, 1979.

---. "Kenneth Burke's Way of Knowing." *Critical Inquiry* 1 (1974): 1-22.

Boyle, Anthony T. "The Epistemological Evolution of Renaissance Utopian Literature: 1516-1657." Diss. New York U, 1983.

Brée, Germaine. *Women Writers in France: Variations on a Theme*. New Brunswick: Rutgers UP, 1973.

Brody, Jane. "Heart Attacks: Turmoil beneath the Calm." *New York Times* 21 June 1983, late ed.: C1+.

Carnegie Council on Policy Studies in Higher Education. *Giving Youth a Better Chance: Options for Education, Work, and Service*. San Francisco: Jossey, 1980.

Cassirer, Ernst. *The Philosophy of Symbolic Forms*. Trans. Ralph Manheim. 3 vols. New Haven: Yale UP, 1955.

Curley, Michael, trans. *Physiologus*. Austin: U of Texas P, 1979.

Frye, Northrop. *Anatomy of Criticism: Four Essays*. Princeton: Princeton UP, 1957.

National Committee on Careers for Older Americans. *Older Americans: An Untapped Resource*. Washington: Acad. for Educ. Dev., 1979.

Potter, G. R., et al. *The New Cambridge Modern History*. 14

vols. Cambridge: Cambridge UP, 1957-70.

Rey-Flaud, Henri. _Pour une dramaturgie du Moyen Age_. Paris:

   PUF, 1980.

Stratman, Carl J., comp. and ed. _Bibliography of English_

   Printed Tragedy, 1565-1900. Carbondale: Southern

   Illinois UP, 1966.

Wellek, René, and Austin Warren. _Theory of Literature_. 3rd

   ed. New York: Harcourt, 1962.

5.5.10. Citing a book without page numbers but with signatures

Some books published before 1800 lack page numbers but include at the foot of every fourth page, or every eighth page, or every sixteenth page, and so on, a letter, numeral, or other symbol, called a signature. These notations were intended to help the bookbinder assemble groups of pages into the proper order. The pages following each new signature may bear the same symbol with an added numeral (either arabic or roman).

In citing books without page numbers but with signatures, treat the signature like a page number. After the author's name, indicate the signature symbol and the leaf number. If no number is printed, supply one: the leaf on which a given signature first appears should be considered "1," the next leaf "2," and so forth, until you reach a new signature. The front of a leaf—that appearing on the reader's right—is considered the "recto" ("r"); the back of the leaf—that appearing on the reader's left—is considered the "verso" ("v"). (On citing books published before 1900, see 4.5.24.)

John Udall, paraphrasing Satan's temptation of Christ, writes,

"throw thy selfe downe" so that "the men of Jerusalem" will

"receive thee with a common applause" (E7v).

Work Cited

Udall, John. The Combate betweene Christ and the Devill: Four

Sermones on the Temptations of Christ. London, 1589.

5.6.   Using notes with parenthetical documentation

The following types of notes may be used with parenthetical documentation:

1. Content notes offering the reader comment, explanation, or information that the text cannot accommodate

2. Bibliographic notes containing either several sources or evaluative comments on sources

In providing this sort of supplementary information, place a superscript arabic numeral at the appropriate place in the text (see 5.8.2) and write the note after a matching numeral either at the end of the text (an endnote) or at the bottom of the page (a footnote) (see 5.8.4).

5.6.1.   Content notes

Avoid essaylike notes, which divert the reader's attention from the primary text. In general, if you cannot fit comments into the text, omit them unless they are essential to justify or clarify what you have written. You may use a note, for example, to explain an unusual citation form, to give the original of a passage translated in the text, or to document an original work that you cite from an indirect source and perhaps to explain its unavailability.

Other interesting and enlightening examples occur in the

stories of Frate Alberto (4.2) and of Madonna Oretta (6.1).[1]

Lionardo Salviati concedes, however, that the <u>Decameron</u> is so
excellent in prose that its author would seriously have erred
had he employed verse.[2]

The remarks of Bernardo Segni and Lionardo Salviati
demonstrate that they were not faithful disciples of
Aristotle.[3]

Notes

[1] The following practice is used in references to tales:
for works that present tales assigned to specific days of a
frame story, the day number is followed by a period and the
tale number (1.4); for works that have no frame tales but were
published in more than one volume, the volume number is
followed by a colon and the tale number (1: 4); and for
single-volume works that number tales consecutively, only the
tale number is given.

[2] ". . . e guai all'Autore, se l'hauesse fatto in versj"
(qtd. in Weinberg 1: 617).

[3] Bernardo Segni, <u>Rettorica et poetica d'Aristotile</u>
(Firenze, 1549), 281, qtd. in Weinberg 1: 405; Lionardo
Salviati, <u>Poetica d'Aristotile parafrasata e comentata</u>
(Firenze, 1586), ms. 2.2.11, Bibl. Naz. Centrale, Firenze,
140v, qtd. in Weinberg 1: 616-17.

For more information on using notes for documentation purposes, see 5.8.

Work Cited

Weinberg, Bernard. A History of Literary Criticism in the

    Italian Renaissance. 2 vols. Chicago: U of Chicago P,

    1961.

5.6.2. Bibliographic notes

Use notes for evaluative comments on sources and for references containing numerous citations.

For older people, the past decade has represented the best of times and the worst of times.[1]

It is a difficult task to attempt to chart the development of drama in the context of medieval and Renaissance Europe.[2]

Notes

[1] For contrasting points of view, see National Committee and Brody C5.

[2] For a sampling of useful source materials, see Potter et al. 1: 176-202; Bondanella and Bondanella, "Lauda"; Rey-Flaud 37-43, 187-201; and Stratman.

Works Cited

Bondanella, Peter, and Julia Conaway Bondanella, eds.

    Dictionary of Italian Literature. Westport: Greenwood,

    1979.

Brody, Jane. "Heart Attacks: Turmoil beneath the Calm." New

York Times 21 June 1983, late ed.: C1+.

National Committee on Careers for Older Americans. Older

Americans: An Untapped Resource. Washington: Acad. for

Educ. Dev., 1979.

Potter, G. R., et al. The New Cambridge Modern History. 14

vols. Cambridge: Cambridge UP, 1957-70.

Rey-Flaud, Henri. Pour une dramaturgie du Moyen Age. Paris:

PUF, 1980.

Stratman, Carl J., comp. and ed. Bibliography of English

Printed Tragedy, 1565-1900. Carbondale: Southern

Illinois UP, 1966.

5.7.   Other types of parenthetical documentation

Other types of parenthetical documentation include the author-date
system (5.7.1), the number system (5.7.2), and complete citations in the
text (5.7.3).

5.7.1.   Author-date system

In the author-date system, the most common in the social and physical sciences, a parenthetical reference includes the author's last name and
the year of publication (unless given in the text), followed by a comma
and the page reference: (Wilson 1982, 73). Information cited in the text
is omitted from the parenthetical reference.

This system also requires a slight change in bibliographic form to assist the reader in finding the appropriate entry in the list of works cited:
the year of publication immediately follows the author's name, and the
title of the work and the remaining publication information complete the

entry. If the list includes more than one work by an author, the entries
are arranged chronologically. If two or more works by the same author
were published in the same year, their order is alphabetical, and the dates
are assigned lowercase letters: 1979a, 1979b.

In The Age of Voltaire the Durants portray eighteenth-century

England as a "humble satellite" in the world of music and art

(1965, 214-48).

The alazon is a "self-deceiving or self-deceived character in

fiction" (Frye 1957a, 365).

Daiches is useful on the Restoration (1970, 2: 538-89), as he

is on other periods.

As Katharina M. Wilson has written, "Intended or not, the

echoes of Tertullian's exhortations in the Utopia provide yet

another level of ambiguity to More's ironic commentary on

social and moral conditions both in sixteenth-century Europe

and in Nowhere-Land" (1982, 73).

There are several excellent essays in the volume Sound and

Poetry (Frye 1957b).

To Will and Ariel Durant, creative men and women make "history

forgivable by enriching our heritage and our lives" (1977,

406).

Works Cited

Daiches, David. 1970. A Critical History of English

Literature. 2nd ed. 2 vols. New York: Ronald.

Durant, Will, and Ariel Durant. 1965. The Age of Voltaire.

New York: Simon. Vol. 9 of The Story of Civilization.

11 vols. 1935-75.

---. 1977. A Dual Autobiography. New York: Simon.

Frye, Northrop. 1957a. Anatomy of Criticism: Four Essays.

Princeton: Princeton UP.

---, ed. 1957b. Sound and Poetry. New York: Columbia UP.

Wilson, Katharina M. 1982. "Tertullian's De cultu

foeminarum and Utopia." Moreana 73: 69-74.

5.7.2.   Number system

In the number system, an arabic numeral designates each entry in the list of works cited and appears in parenthetical documentation (sometimes underlined) along with the page reference, which follows a comma. The year of publication remains at the end of the bibliographic entry, and the list may follow any useful order. (In the sciences, for example, the works cited are frequently listed in the order in which they are first mentioned in the text.)

The alazon is a "self-deceiving or self-deceived character in

fiction" (2, 365).

In The Age of Voltaire the Durants portray eighteenth-century

England as a "humble satellite" in the world of music and art

(1, 214-48).

There are several excellent essays in the volume <u>Sound and Poetry</u> (<u>3</u>).

Works Cited

1. Durant, Will, and Ariel Durant. <u>The Age of Voltaire</u>. New
York: Simon, 1965. Vol. 9 of <u>The Story of Civilization</u>.
11 vols. 1935-75.

2. Frye, Northrop. <u>Anatomy of Criticism: Four Essays</u>.
Princeton: Princeton UP, 1957.

3. ---, ed. <u>Sound and Poetry</u>. New York: Columbia UP, 1957.

5.7.3.   Complete citations in the text

The practice of placing full publication information in parenthetical references is seldom followed, because it deprives the reader of the benefits of a list of works cited and interrupts the flow of the text. It is sometimes adopted, however, in bibliographic studies or in works requiring few references. As in other systems, information given in the text is not repeated in the reference. Commas replace separating periods and square brackets are used for parentheses within parentheses.

The <u>alazon</u>, as Northrop Frye describes it, is a "self-deceiving or self-deceived character in fiction" (<u>Anatomy of Criticism: Four Essays</u>, Princeton: Princeton UP, 1957, 365).

In <u>A Critical History of English Literature</u> David Daiches is useful on the Restoration (2nd ed., 2 vols., New York: Ronald, 1970, 2: 538-89), as he is on other periods.

5.8.   Using notes for documentation

Another system of documentation entails using endnotes or footnotes to cite sources.

5.8.1.   Documentation notes versus the list of works cited and parenthetical references

Publications that print documentation notes usually do not include a list of works cited. first note references include the publication information found in a bibliographic entry—the author's name, the title, and the publication facts—as well as the specific page reference. (Subsequent references to a work require less information; see 5.8.8.) Note form, however, differs slightly from bibliographic form (see 5.8.3), and note numbers replace parenthetical references at appropriate points in the text to draw the reader's attention to citations (see 5.8.2). Documentation notes appear either at the end of the text, as endnotes, or at the bottoms of relevant pages, as footnotes (see 5.8.4).

5.8.2.   Note numbers

Notes are numbered consecutively, starting from 1, throughout an essay or, usually, a chapter in a book, except for any notes accompanying special material, such as a figure or a table (see 3.4). They are not numbered by individual pages or indicated by asterisks or other symbols. Note numbers are "superior" or "superscript" figures—arabic numerals typed slightly above the line, like this[1]—without periods, parentheses, or slashes. They follow punctuation marks except dashes and occasionally parentheses. (When the note is to only the material that appears within parentheses, the note number is placed before the closing parenthesis.) In general, a note number, like a parenthetical reference, is placed where it will prove least disruptive—usually at the end of the sentence, clause, or phrase containing the material documented.

5.8.3.   Note form versus bibliographic form

With some exceptions, documentary notes and bibliographic entries provide the same information but differ in form.

Bibliography form

A bibliographic entry has three main divisions, each followed by a period: the author's name reversed for alphabetizing, the title, and the publishing data.

Frye, Northrop. Anatomy of Criticism: Four Essays.

     Princeton: Princeton UP, 1957.

Note form

A documentary note has four main divisions, with a period only at the end: the author's name in normal order, followed by a comma; the title; the publishing data (in parentheses for citations of books); and a page reference.

     [1] Northrop Frye, Anatomy of Criticism: Four Essays

(Princeton: Princeton UP, 1957) 52.

5.8.4.   Endnotes and footnotes

In preparing a manuscript for publication, make all notes endnotes. As their name implies, endnotes appear after the text, starting on a new page numbered in sequence with the preceding page. Center the title "Notes" one inch from the top, double-space, indent five spaces from the left margin, and type the note number, without punctuation, slightly above the line. Leave a space and type the reference. If the note extends to two or more lines, begin subsequent lines at the left margin. Type the notes consecutively, double-spaced, and number all pages.

In dissertations, notes usually appear at the bottoms of pages, beginning four lines (two double spaces) below the text. Single-space footnotes but double-space between them. When a note continues on the following page, type a solid line across the new page one line (one double space) below the last line of the text and continue the note four lines (a total of two double spaces) below the text. Footnotes for the new page immediately follow the note continued from the previous page. (See also ch. 7, on preparing theses and dissertations.)

5.8.5.   Sample first note references: Books

Bibliographic entries corresponding to the following sample notes appear in the sections indicated in parentheses after the headings. Consult the appropriate section if you need additional information on citing a particular type of reference.

a.   A book by a single author (4.5.1)

¹ Vivian R. Pollak, Dickinson: The Anxiety of Gender (Ithaca: Cornell UP, 1984) 32.

b.   An anthology or a compilation (4.5.2)

² Fred J. Nichols, ed. and trans., An Anthology of Neo-Latin Poetry (New Haven: Yale UP, 1979) vii-viii.

c.   A book by two or more persons (4.5.4)

³ Clyde E. Blocker, Robert H. Plummer, and Richard C. Richardson, Jr., The Two-Year College: A Social Synthesis (Englewood Cliffs: Prentice, 1965) 52-57.

d.   A book by a corporate author (4.5.6)

⁴ Commission on the Humanities, The Humanities in American Life: Report of the Commission on the Humanities (Berkeley: U of California P, 1980) 69.

e.   An anonymous book (4.5.7)

⁵ A Handbook of Korea, 4th ed. (Seoul: Korean Overseas Information Service, Ministry of Culture and Information, 1982) 241-47.

f. A work in an anthology (4.5.8)

[6] Gabriel García Márquez, "A Very Old Man with Enormous Wings," "Leaf Storm" and Other Stories, trans. Gregory Rabassa (New York: Harper, 1972) 105.

[7] Lorraine Hansberry, A Raisin in the Sun, Black Theater: A Twentieth-Century Collection of the Work of Its Best Playwrights, ed. Lindsay Patterson (New York: Dodd, 1971) 265-76.

g. An introduction, preface, foreword, or afterword (4.5.9)

[8] Edgar Johnson, afterword, David Copperfield, by Charles Dickens (New York: Signet-NAL, 1962) 875.

h. A multivolume work (4.5.11)

[9] David Daiches, A Critical History of English Literature, 2nd ed., 2 vols. (New York: Ronald, 1970) 2: 538-39.

[10] Arthur M. Schlesinger, gen. ed., History of U.S. Political Parties, 4 vols. (New York: Chelsea, 1973) vol. 4.

i. An "edition" (4.5.12)

[11] Geoffrey Chaucer, The Works of Geoffrey Chaucer, ed. F. N. Robinson, 2nd ed. (Boston: Houghton, 1957) 545.

¹² Jo Ann Boydston, ed., <u>Psychology</u>, by John Dewey
(Carbondale: Southern Illinois UP, 1967) 85-87, vol. 2 of <u>John
Dewey: The Early Works, 1882-1898</u>.

j. A translation (4.5.13)

¹³ Feodor Dostoevsky, <u>Crime and Punishment</u>, trans. Jessie
Coulson, ed. George Gibian (New York: Norton, 1964) 157.

¹⁴ Joseph G. Fucilla, trans., <u>Three Melodramas</u>, by Pietro
Metastasio, Studies in Romances Langs. 24 (Lexington: UP of
Kentucky, 1981) 1-14.

k. A republished book (4.5.14)

¹⁵ E. L. Doctorow, <u>Welcome to Hard Times</u> (1960; New York:
Bantam, 1976) 209-12.

l. An article in a reference book (4.5.15)

¹⁶ "Mandarin," <u>Encyclopedia Americana</u>, 1980 ed.

m. A pamphlet (4.5.16)

¹⁷ Weldon A. Kefauver, ed., <u>Scholars and Their
Publishers</u> (New York: MLA, 1977).

n.   A government publication (4.5.17)

[18] United Nations, Economic Commission for Africa, Industrial Growth in Africa (New York: United Nations, 1963) 4-6.

o.   A book in a series (4.5.18)

[19] Isidore Silver, Ronsard and the Grecian Lyre, Travaux d'humanisme et Renaissance 12 (Genève: Droz, 1981) 62.

p.   A publisher's imprint (4.5.19)

[20] Leo Tolstoy, The Kingdom of God Is within You, trans. Constance Garnett (Lincoln: Bison-U of Nebraska P, 1984) 206.

q.   A book with multiple publishers (4.5.20)

[21] J. Wight Duff, A Literary History of Rome: From the Origins to the Close of the Golden Age, ed. A. M. Duff, 3rd ed. (1953; London: Benn; New York: Barnes, 1967) 88.

r.   Published proceedings of a conference (4.5.21)

[22] Alan M. Gordon and Evelyn Rugg, eds., Actas del Sexto Congreso Internacional de Hispanistas celebrado en Toronto del 22 al 26 agosto 1977 (Toronto: Dept. of Spanish and Portuguese, U of Toronto, 1980) v-vii.

s. A book in a language other than English (4.5.22)

[23] Barbara Wachowicz, Marie jeho života (Praha
[Prague]: Lidové, 1979) 1-15.

t. A book with a title within its title (4.5.23)

[24] Leonard Mades, The Armor and the Brocade: A Study of
Don Quijote and The Courtier (New York: Las Americas, 1968)
5-11.

u. A book published before 1900 (4.5.24)

[25] John Dewey, The Study of Ethics: A Syllabus (Ann
Arbor, 1894) 104.

v. A book without stated publication information or pagination (4.5.25)

[26] Zvi Malachi, ed., Proceedings of the International
Conference on Literary and Linguistic Computing ([Tel Aviv]:
[Tel Aviv U Fac. of Humanities], n.d.) 1-3.

w. An unpublished dissertation (4.5.26)

[27] Nancy Kay Johnson, "Cultural and Psychosocial
Determinants of Health and Illness," diss., U of Washington,
1980, 34.

x.   A published dissertation (4.5.27)

²⁸ Rudolf E. Dietze, <u>Ralph Ellison: The Genesis of an</u>
<u>Artist</u>, diss., U Erlangen-Nürnberg, 1982, Erlanger Beiträge
zur Sprach- und Kunstwissenschaft 70 (Nürnberg: Carl, 1982)
168.

5.8.6.   Sample first note references: Articles in periodicals

For additional information on citing the following types of sources, consult the related sections for bibliographic entries, indicated in parentheses after the headings.

a.   An article in a journal with continuous pagination (4.7.1)

¹ Karen Spear, "Building Cognitive Skills in Basic
Writers," <u>Teaching English in the Two-Year College</u> 9 (1983):
94.

b.   An article in a journal that pages each issue separately or that uses only issue numbers (4.7.2)

² Frederick Barthelme, "Architecture," <u>Kansas Quarterly</u>
13.3-4 (1981): 77-78.

³ Allan Pritchard, "West of the Great Divide: A View of
the Literature of British Columbia," <u>Canadian Literature</u> 94
(1982): 100-01.

c. An article from a journal with more than one series (4.7.3)

[4] Robert Avery, "Foreign Influence on the Nautical Terminology of Russian in the Eighteenth Century," Oxford Slavonic Papers ns 14 (1981): 83.

[5] Michael P. Johnson, "Runaway Slaves and the Slave Committees in South Carolina, 1799-1830," William and Mary Quarterly 3rd ser. 38 (1981): 438-41.

d. An article from a weekly or biweekly periodical (4.7.4)

[6] Kim McDonald, "Space Shuttle Columbia's Weightless Laboratory Attracts Research," Chronicle of Higher Education 28 Oct. 1981: 6.

e. An article from a monthly or bimonthly periodical (4.7.5)

[7] Mark Snyder, "Self-Fulfilling Stereotypes," Psychology Today July 1982: 68.

f. An article from a daily newspaper (4.7.6)

[8] Jane Brody, "Heart Attacks: Turmoil beneath the Calm," New York Times 21 June 1983, late ed.: C1.

g. An editorial (4.7.7)

[9] Morton Malkofsky, "Let the Unions Negotiate What's Negotiable," editorial, Learning Oct. 1982: 6.

h. An anonymous article (4.7.8)

[10] "Portents for Future Learning," Time 21 Sept. 1981: 65.

i. A letter to the editor (4.7.9)

[11] Harry Levin, letter, Partisan Review 47 (1980): 320.

j. A review (4.7.10)

[12] John Updike, "Cohn's Doom," rev. of God's Grace, by Bernard Malamud, New Yorker 8 Nov. 1982: 169.

[13] Sherley Ashton, rev. of Death and Dying, by David L. Bender and Richard C. Hagen, Humanist July-Aug. 1982: 60.

[14] "The Cooling of an Admiration," rev. of Pound/Joyce: The Letters of Ezra Pound to James Joyce, ed. Forrest Read, Times Literary Supplement 6 Mar. 1969: 239-40.

[15] Rev. of Anthology of Danish Literature, ed. F. J. Billeskov Jansen and P. M. Mitchell, Times Literary Supplement 7 July 1972: 785.

k.   An article whose title contains a quotation or a title within quotation marks (4.7.11)

[16] E. E. Duncan-Jones, "Moore's 'A Kiss à l'Antique' and Keats's 'Ode on a Grecian Urn,'" Notes and Queries ns 28 (1981): 316-17.

l.   An article from *Dissertation Abstracts* or *Dissertation Abstracts International* (4.7.12)

[17] Nancy Kay Johnson, "Cultural and Psychosocial Determinants of Health and Illness," DAI 40 (1980): 4235B (U of Washington).

m.   A serialized article (4.7.13)

[18] Harrison T. Meserole and James M. Rambeau, "Articles on American Literature Appearing in Current Periodicals," American Literature 52 (1981): 688-90; 53 (1981): 164-66, 348-52.

[19] Martin Gottlieb, "Times Square Development Plan: A Lesson in Politics and Power," New York Times 9 Mar. 1984, late ed.: B1; "Pressure and Compromise Saved Times Square Project," New York Times 10 Mar. 1984, late ed.: 25.

n.   A special issue of a journal (4.7.14)

[20] W. J. T. Mitchell, ed., The Politics of

<u>Interpretation</u>, spec. issue of <u>Critical Inquiry</u> 9.1 (1982):
1-278 (Chicago: U of Chicago P, 1983).

[21] <u>Picaresque Tradition</u>, spec. issue of <u>College</u>
<u>Literature</u> 6.3 (1979): 165-270.

[22] Paula Gunn Allen, "'The Grace That Remains': American
Indian Women's Literature," <u>American Indians Today: Their</u>
<u>Thought, Their Literature, Their Art</u>, ed. Elaine Jahner, spec.
issue of <u>Book Forum</u> 5.3 (1981): 382.

5.8.7.   Sample first references: Other sources

For additional information on the following types of documentation,
consult the related sections for bibliographic entries, indicated in parentheses after the headings.

a.   Computer software (4.8.1)

[1] <u>Wordstar</u>, release 3.3, computer software, Micropro,
1983.

[2] Richard E. Pattis, <u>Karel the Robot: A Gentle</u>
<u>Introduction to the Art of Programming</u>, computer software,
Cybertronics, 1981.

b.   Material from a computer service (4.8.2)

[3] Howard Schomer, "South Africa: Beyond Fair Employment,"
<u>Harvard Business Review</u> May-June 1983: 145+ (DIALOG file 122,
item 119425 833160).

[4] "Barbara Bush Turner," American Men and Women of
Science, 15th ed. (Bowker, 1983) (DIALOG file 236, item
0107406).

c. Material from an information service (4.8.3)

[5] Bernard Spolsky, Navajo Language Maintenance: Six-Year-
Olds in 1969, Navajo Reading Study Prog. Rept. 5 (Albuquerque:
U of New Mexico, 1969) 22 (ERIC ED 043 044).

[6] Paul R. Streiff, Some Criteria for Designing Evaluation
of TESOL Programs (ERIC, 1970) 10 (ED 040 385).

d. Radio and television programs (4.8.4)

[7] "The Joy Ride," writ. Alfred Shaughnessy, Upstairs,
Downstairs, created by Eileen Atkins and Jean Marsh, dir. Bill
Bain, prod. John Hawkesworth, Masterpiece Theatre, introd.
Alistair Cooke, PBS, WGBH, Boston, 6 Feb. 1977.

e. Recordings (4.8.5)

[8] Wolfgang A. Mozart, Symphony no. 35 in D and Overtures
to The Marriage of Figaro, The Magic Flute, and Don Giovanni,
cond. Antonia Brico, Mostly Mozart Orch., Columbia, M33888,
1979.

[9] Robert Frost, "The Road Not Taken," Robert Frost Reads
His Poetry, Caedmon, TC 1060, 1956.

[10] D. K. Wilgus, Southern Folk Tales, audiotape, rec. 23-25 Mar. 1965, U of California, Los Angeles, Archives of Folklore, B.76.82 (7 1/2 ips, 7" reel).

[11] David Lewiston, jacket notes, The Balinese Gamelan: Music from the Morning of the World, Nonesuch Explorer Series, H-2015, n.d.

f. Films, filmstrips, slide programs, and videotapes (4.8.6)

[12] Det Sjunde Inseglet [The Seventh Seal], dir. Ingmar Bergman, Svensk Filmindustri, 1956.

[13] Consumer Awareness: Supply, Demand, Competition, and Prices, sound filmstrip, prod. Visual Education, Maclean Hunter Learning Resources, 1981 (85 fr., 11 min.).

g. Performances (4.8.7)

[14] George Balanchine, chor., Mozartiana, with Suzanne Farrell, New York City Ballet, New York State Theater, 20 Nov. 1981.

[15] Scott Joplin, Treemonisha, dir. Frank Corsaro, cond. Gunther Schuller, with Carmen Balthrop, Betty Allen, and Curtis Rayam, Houston Grand Opera, Miller Theatre, Houston, 18 May 1975.

h. Musical compositions (4.8.8)

[16] Ludwig van Beethoven, Symphony no. 7 in A, op. 92.

i. Works of art (4.8.9)

[17] Rembrandt van Rijn, <u>Aristotle Contemplating the Bust</u> <u>of Homer</u>, Metropolitan Museum of Art, New York.

[18] Mary Cassatt, <u>Mother and Child</u>, Wichita Art Museum, Wichita, slide 22 of <u>American Painting: 1560-1913</u>, by John Pearce (New York: McGraw, 1964).

j. Letters (4.8.10)

[19] William Makepeace Thackeray, "To George Henry Lewes," 6 Mar. 1848, letter 452 of <u>Letters and Private Papers of</u> <u>William Makepeace Thackeray</u>, ed. Gordon N. Ray, 4 vols. (Cambridge: Harvard UP, 1945-46) 2: 353-54.

[20] Thomas Hart Benton, letter to John Charles Fremont, 22 June 1847, John Charles Fremont Papers, Southwest Museum Library, Los Angeles.

[21] Aaron Copland, letter to the author, 17 May 1982.

k. Interviews (4.8.11)

[22] Federico Fellini, "The Long Interview," <u>Juliet of the</u> <u>Spirits</u>, ed. Tullio Kezich, trans. Howard Greenfield (New York: Ballantine, 1966) 56.

[23] Suzanne Gordon, interview, <u>All Things Considered</u>, Natl. Public Radio, WNYC, New York, 1 June 1983.

[24] I. M. Pei, personal interview, 27 July 1983.

l. Maps and charts (4.8.12)

^{25} Canada, map (Chicago: Rand, 1983).

^{26} Grammar and Punctuation, chart (Grand Haven: School Zone, 1980).

m. Cartoons (4.8.13)

^{27} Charles Schulz, "Peanuts," cartoon, Star-Ledger [Newark, NJ] 4 Sept. 1980: 72.

^{28} Charles Addams, cartoon, New Yorker 21 Feb. 1983: 41.

n. Lectures, speeches, and addresses (4.8.14)

^{29} Florence Ridley, "Forget the Past, Reject the Future: Chaos Is Come Again," Div. on Teaching of Literature, MLA Convention, Los Angeles, 28 Dec. 1982.

^{30} John Ciardi, address, Opening General Sess., NCTE Convention, Washington, 19 Nov. 1982.

o. Manuscripts and typescripts (4.8.15)

^{31} Mark Twain, Notebook 32, ts., Mark Twain Papers, U of California, Berkeley, 50.

p. Legal references (4.8.16)

^{32} Stevens v. National Broadcasting Co., 148 USPQ 755 (Calif. Super. Ct. 1966).

5.8.8. Subsequent references

Once a work has been fully documented, subsequent notes give only enough information to identify the work (see 5.3). The author's last name alone, followed by the relevant page numbers, is usually adequate.

[4] Frye 345-47.

If two or more works by the same author are cited — for example, Northrop Frye's *Anatomy of Criticism* as well as his *Critical Path* — a shortened form of the title should follow the author's last name in references after the first.

[8] Frye, Anatomy 278.

[9] Frye, Critical 1-10.

The information is repeated even when two references in sequence refer to the same work. "Ibid." and "op. cit." are no longer used.

5.9. Other style manuals

Every scholarly field has its preferred format or "style." MLA style, as presented in this manual, is widely accepted in humanities disciplines. The following manuals describe the styles of other disciplines:

Biology

Council of Biology Editors. Style Manual Committee. *CBE Style Manual: A Guide for Authors, Editors, and Publishers in the Biological Sciences.* 5th ed. Bethesda: Council of Biology Editors, 1983.

Chemistry

American Chemical Society. *Handbook for Authors of Papers in American Chemical Society Publications.* Washington: Amer. Chemical Soc., 1978.

Geology

United States. Geological Survey. *Suggestions to Authors of the Reports of the United States Geological Survey.* 6th ed. Washington: GPO, 1978.

Linguistics

Linguistic Society of America. *LSA Bulletin*, Dec. issue, annually.

Mathematics

American Mathematical Society. *A Manual for Authors of Mathematical Papers.* 7th ed. Providence: Amer. Mathematical Soc., 1980.

Medicine

International Steering Committee of Medical Editors. "Uniform Requirements for Manuscripts Submitted to Biomedical Journals." *Annals of Internal Medicine* 90 (Jan. 1979): 95–99.

Physics

American Institute of Physics. Publications Board. *Style Manual for Guidance in the Preparation of Papers.* 3rd ed. New York: Amer. Inst. of Physics, 1978.

Psychology

American Psychological Association. *Publication Manual of the American Psychological Association.* 3rd ed. Washington: Amer. Psychological Assn., 1983.

Other available style manuals are addressed primarily to editors and concern procedures for converting a manuscript into type:

The Chicago Manual of Style. 13th ed. Chicago: U of Chicago P, 1982.

Ostermann, Georg F. von. *Manual of Foreign Languages: For the Use of Librarians, Bibliographers, Research Workers, Editors, Translators, and Printers.* 4th ed. New York: Central, 1952.

United States. Government Printing Office. *Style Manual.* Rev. ed. Washington: GPO, 1973.

Words into Type. By Marjorie E. Skillin, Robert M. Gay, et al. 3rd ed. Englewood Cliffs: Prentice, 1974.

For other style manuals and authors' guides, see John Bruce Howell, *Style Manuals of the English-Speaking World* (Phoenix: Oryx, 1983).

6 ABBREVIATIONS, REFERENCE WORDS, PROOFREADING SYMBOLS

6.1. Introduction

Abbreviations are commonly used in the list of works cited and in tabular material but rarely in the text of a scholarly manuscript (except within parentheses). In choosing abbreviations, keep your audience in mind. While economy of space is important, clarity is more so. Spell out a term if the abbreviation may puzzle your readers.

When abbreviating, always use commonly accepted forms. In appropriate contexts, you may abbreviate days, months, and other measurements of time (see 6.2); states and countries (see 6.3); terms and reference words common in scholarship (see 6.4); publishers' names (see 6.5); literary and religious works (see 6.6); and languages (see 6.7).

The trend in abbreviation is to use neither periods after letters nor spaces between letters, especially for abbreviations made up of all capital letters.

```
BC    NJ    PhD   S
```

The chief exception to this trend continues to be the initials used for personal names: a period and a space ordinarily follow each initial.

```
H. L. Mencken
```

Likewise, most abbreviations that end in lowercase letters are followed by periods.

```
assn.     Eng.     fig.
introd.   Mex.     prod.
```

Whenever such an abbreviation is part of a longer one, the other parts also take periods and spaces.

```
H. Doc.   n. pag.   U. S. Dept. of Labor
```

In most abbreviations made up of single lowercase letters, a period follows each letter, with no spaces between letters.

```
a.m.   e.g.   i.e.   n.p.
```

But there are numerous exceptions.

```
ips    ns     os     rpm
```

6.2. Time

Spell out the names of months in the text but abbreviate them in documentation, except for May, June, and July. Whereas words denoting units of time are also spelled out in the text (seconds, minutes, weeks, months, years, centuries), some time designations are used *only* in abbreviated form (a.m., p.m., AD, BC, BCE, CE).

AD	*anno Domini* 'in the year of the Lord' (used before numerals: AD 14)
a.m.	*ante meridiem* 'before noon'
Apr.	April
Aug.	August
BC	before Christ (used after numerals: 19 BC)
BCE	before the Common Era
CE	Common Era
cent., cents.	century, centuries
Dec.	December
Feb.	February
Fri.	Friday

hr., hrs.	hour, hours
Jan.	January
Mar.	March
min., mins.	minute, minutes
mo., mos.	month, months
Mon.	Monday
Nov.	November
Oct.	October
p.m.	*post meridiem* 'after noon'
Sat.	Saturday
sec., secs.	second, seconds
Sept.	September
Sun.	Sunday
Thurs.	Thursday
Tues.	Tuesday
Wed.	Wednesday
wk., wks.	week, weeks
yr., yrs.	year, years

6.3.   Geographical names

Spell out the names of states, territories, and possessions of the United States in the text, except, usually, in addresses and sometimes in parentheses. Likewise, spell out in the text the names of countries, with a few exceptions (e.g., USSR, BRD, DDR). In documentation, however, abbreviate the names of states, provinces, and countries.

AB	Alberta
AK	Alaska
AL	Alabama
Alb.	Albania
AR	Arkansas
Arg.	Argentina
Arm.	Armenia
AS	American Samoa
Aus.	Austria
Austral.	Australia
AZ	Arizona

BC	British Columbia
Belg.	Belgium
Braz.	Brazil
BRD	Bundesrepublik Deutschland (W. Ger.)
Bulg.	Bulgaria
CA	California
Can.	Canada
CO	Colorado
CT	Connecticut
CZ	Canal Zone
Czech.	Czechoslovakia
DC	District of Columbia
DDR	Deutsche Demokratische Republik (E. Ger.)
DE	Delaware
Den.	Denmark
Ecua.	Ecuador
E. Ger.	East Germany (DDR)
Eng.	England
FL	Florida
Fr.	France
GA	Georgia
Gr.	Greece
Gt. Brit.	Great Britain
GU	Guam
HI	Hawaii
Hung.	Hungary
IA	Iowa
ID	Idaho
IL	Illinois
IN	Indiana
Ire.	Ireland
Isr.	Israel
It.	Italy
Jap.	Japan
KS	Kansas
KY	Kentucky
LA	Louisiana
LB	Labrador
Leb.	Lebanon
MA	Massachusetts
MB	Manitoba
MD	Maryland

ME	Maine
Mex.	Mexico
MI	Michigan
MN	Minnesota
MO	Missouri
MS	Mississippi
MT	Montana
NB	New Brunswick
NC	North Carolina
ND	North Dakota
NE	Nebraska
Neth.	Netherlands
NF	Newfoundland
NH	New Hampshire
NJ	New Jersey
NM	New Mexico
Norw.	Norway
NS	Nova Scotia
NT	Northwest Territories
NV	Nevada
NY	New York
NZ	New Zealand
OH	Ohio
OK	Oklahoma
ON	Ontario
OR	Oregon
PA	Pennsylvania
Pan.	Panama
PE	Prince Edward Island
Pol.	Poland
Port.	Portugal
PQ	Québec (Province de Québec)
PR	Puerto Rico
PRC	People's Republic of China
RI	Rhode Island
S. Afr.	South Africa
SC	South Carolina
Scot.	Scotland
SD	South Dakota
SK	Saskatchewan
Sp.	Spain
Swed.	Sweden

Switz.	Switzerland
TN	Tennessee
TX	Texas
Turk.	Turkey
UK	United Kingdom
US, USA	United States, United States of America
USSR	Union of Soviet Socialist Republics
UT	Utah
VA	Virginia
VI	Virgin Islands
VT	Vermont
WA	Washington
W. Ger.	West Germany (BRD)
WI	Wisconsin
WV	West Virginia
WY	Wyoming
YT	Yukon Territory
Yug.	Yugoslavia

6.4.   Common scholarly abbreviations and reference words

The following list includes both abbreviations and reference words commonly used in humanities research studies. Abbreviations within parentheses are alternative, but not preferred, forms. Abbreviations within square brackets are no longer recommended. Most of the abbreviations listed would replace the spelled forms only in parentheses, tabular material, or documentation.

[a.a.O.]	Ger. *am angeführten Orte* 'in the place cited'
AB	*Artium Baccalaureus* 'Bachelor of Arts'
abbr.	abbreviation, abbreviated
abl.	ablative
abr.	abridged, abridgment
acad.	academy
acc.	accusative
act.	active
adapt.	adapted by, adaptation
adj.	adjective

adv.	adverb
als	autograph letter signed
AM	*Artium Magister* 'Master of Arts'
Anm.	Ger. *Anmerkung* 'note'
anon.	anonymous
ant.	antonym
[ante]	'before'
app.	appendix
arch.	archaic
art.	article
assn.	association
assoc.	associate, associated
attrib.	attributed to; attributive
aux.	auxiliary
b.	born
BA	Bachelor of Arts
Bd., Bde.	Ger. *Band, Bände* 'volume(s)'
bib.	biblical
bibliog.	bibliography, bibliographer, bibliographic, bibliographical
biog.	biography, biographer, biographical
bk.	book
BL	British Library, London (formerly British Museum)
BM	British Museum, London (now British Library)
BN	Bibliothèque Nationale, Paris
BS	Bachelor of Science
bull.	bulletin
©	copyright (© 1986)
c. (ca.)	*circa* 'about' (used with approximate dates: c. 1796)
cap.	capital, capitalize
cf.	*confer* 'compare' (*not* 'see')
ch. (chap.)	chapter
chor.	choreographed by, choreographer
cit.	citation, cited
cog.	cognate
col.	column
coll.	college
colloq.	colloquial
comp.	compiled by, compiler
compar.	comparative
cond.	conducted by, conductor
Cong.	Congress

Cong. Rec.	*Congressional Record*
conj.	conjunction
cons.	consonant
Const.	Constitution
cont.	contents; continued
(contd.)	continued
contr.	contraction
d.	died
DA	Doctor of Arts
DA, DAI	*Dissertation Abstracts, Dissertation Abstracts International*
DAB	*Dictionary of American Biography*
dat.	dative
def.	definite
dept.	department
der.	derivative
dev.	developed by, development
d.h.	Ger. *das heisst* 'that is'
dial.	dialect
dim.	diminutive
dir.	directed by, director
diss.	dissertation
dist.	district
distr.	distributed by, distributor
div.	division
DNB	*Dictionary of National Biography*
[ebd.]	Ger. *ebenda* 'in the same place'
ed.	edited by, editor, edition
[ed. cit.]	*editio citata* 'edition cited'
EdD	Doctor of Education
educ.	education, educational
e.g.	*exempli gratia* 'for example' (rarely capitalized; set off by commas, unless preceded by a different punctuation mark)
enl.	enlarged (as in "rev. and enl. ed.")
esp.	especially
et al.	*et alii* 'and others'
etc.	*et cetera* 'and so forth' (like most abbreviations, not appropriate in the text)
[et seq., et seqq.]	*et sequens, et sequentes* or *sequentia* 'and the following'
ex.	example
[f., ff.]	and the following page(s) or line(s)

fac.	faculty
facsim. (facs.)	facsimile
fasc.	fascicle
fem.	feminine
fig.	figure
fl.	*floruit* 'flourished, reached greatest development or influence' (used before dates of historical figures when birth and death dates are not known)
[fn.]	footnote
[fol.]	folio
fr.	from
front.	frontispiece
fut.	future
fwd.	foreword, foreword by
geb.	Ger. *geboren* 'born'
gen.	general (as in "gen. ed.")
ger.	gerund
gest.	Ger. *gestorben* 'died'
govt.	government
GPO	Government Printing Office, Washington, DC
H. Doc.	House [of Representatives] Document
hist.	history, historian, historical
HMSO	Her (His) Majesty's Stationery Office
HR	House of Representatives
H. Rept.	House [of Representatives] Report
H. Res.	House [of Representatives] Resolution
[ib., ibid.]	*ibidem* 'in the same place' (i.e., the single title cited in the note immediately preceding)
i.e.	*id est* 'that is' (rarely capitalized; set off by commas, unless preceded by a different punctuation mark)
illus.	illustrated by, illustrator, illustration
imp.	imperative
imperf.	imperfect
inc.	incorporated; including
indef.	indefinite
indic.	indicative
infin.	infinitive
[infra]	'below'
inst.	institute, institution
interjec.	interjection
interrog.	interrogative
intl.	international

intrans.	intransitive
introd.	(author of) introduction, introduced by, introduction
ips	inches per second (used in reference to recording tapes)
irreg.	irregular
jour.	journal
Jr.	Junior
KB	kilobytes
l., ll.	line, lines (avoided in favor of "line" and "lines" or, if clear, numbers only)
lang.	language
LC	Library of Congress
leg.	legal
legis.	legislation, legislative, legislature, legislator
lit.	literally; literary, literature
LLB	*Legum Baccalaureus* 'Bachelor of Laws'
LLD	*Legum Doctor* 'Doctor of Laws'
[loc. cit.]	*loco citato* 'in the place (passage) cited' (i.e., in the same passage referred to in a recent reference)
ltd.	limited
m.	Fr. *mort, morte*; It. *morto, morta*; Sp. *muerto, muerta* 'died'
MA	Master of Arts
mag.	magazine
masc.	masculine
MD	*Medicinae Doctor* 'Doctor of Medicine'
misc.	miscellaneous
ms., mss.	manuscript, manuscripts
MS	Master of Science
n, nn	note, notes (used immediately after page number: 56n, 56n3, 56nn3–5)
n.	noun. Also Fr. *né, née*; Ital. *nato, nata*; Lat. *natus, nata*; Sp. *nacido, nacida* 'born'
narr.	narrated by, narrator
natl.	national
NB	*nota bene* 'take notice, mark well' (always capitalized)
n.d.	no date (of publication)
NED	*New English Dictionary* (cf. *OED*)
neut.	neuter
no.	number (cf. "numb.")
nom.	nominative
nonstand.	nonstandard

n.p.	no place (of publication); no publisher
n. pag.	no pagination
ns	new series
NS	New Style (calendar)
numb.	numbered
ob.	Lat. *obiit* 'he (she) died'
obj.	object, objective
obs.	obsolete
OED	*Oxford English Dictionary* (formerly *New English Dictionary* [*NED*])
o.J.	Ger. *ohne Jahr* 'without year'
o.O.	Ger. *ohne Ort* 'without place'
op.	opus (work)
[op. cit.]	*opere citato* 'in the work cited'
orch.	orchestra, orchestrated by
orig.	original, originally
orn.	ornament, ornamentation
os	old series; original series
OS	Old Style (calendar)
p., pp.	page, pages (omitted before page numbers unless reference would otherwise be unclear)
P	Press; Fr. *Presse, Presses* (used in documentation; see "UP" and "PU")
pág.	Sp. *página* 'page'
par.	paragraph
part.	participle
pass.	passive
[passim]	'through the work, here and there'
perf.	performer, performed by; perfect
pers.	person
p. es.	It. *per esempio* 'for example'
p. ex.	Fr. *par exemple* 'for example'
PhD	*Philosophiae Doctor* 'Doctor of Philosophy'
philol.	philological
philos.	philosophical
pl.	plate; plural
por ej.	Sp. *por ejemplo* 'for example'
poss.	possessive
[post]	'after'
p.p.	past participle
pref.	preface, preface by
prep.	preposition

pres.	present
proc.	proceedings
prod.	produced by, producer
pron.	pronoun
pronunc.	pronunciation
pr. p.	present participle
PS	postscript
pseud.	pseudonym
pt.	part
PU	Fr. *presses de l'université, presses universitaires*
pub (publ.)	published by, publisher, publication
q.v.	*quod vide* 'which see'
r	*recto* 'righthand page'
r.	reigned
rec.	recorded, record
refl.	reflexive
reg.	registered; regular
rel.	relative
rept.	reported by, report
res.	resolution
resp.	respectively
rev.	revised by, revision; review, reviewed by (spell out "review" where "rev." might be ambiguous)
rpm	revolutions per minute (used in reference to recordings)
rpt.	reprinted by, reprint
s.	Ger. *siehe* 'see'
S	Senate
S.	Ger. *Seite* 'page'
sc.	scene (omitted when act and scene numbers are used together: *Lear* 4.1)
s.d.	Fr. *sans date*, It. *senza data* 'without date'
S. Doc.	Senate Document
sec. (sect.)	section
ser.	series
sess.	session
s.f.	Sp. *sin fecha* 'without date'
sic	'thus, so' (placed within square brackets when used as an editorial interpolation [see 2.6.5], otherwise in parentheses; not followed by an exclamation mark)
sig.	signature

sing.	singular
s.l.	Fr. *sans lieu*, It. *senza luogo*, Sp. *sin lugar* 'without place'
s.l.n.d.	Fr. *sans lieu ni date* 'without place or date'
soc.	society
spec.	special
Sr.	Senior
S. Rept.	Senate Report
S. Res.	Senate Resolution
st.	stanza
St., Sts. (S, SS)	Saint, Saints
Ste, Stes	Fr. fem. *Sainte, Saintes* 'saint(s)'
subj.	subject, subjective; subjunctive
substand.	substandard
superl.	superlative
supp.	supplement
[supra]	*supra* 'above'
s.v.	*sub verbo* or *voce* 'under the word or heading'
syn.	synonym
t.	Fr. *tome*, Sp. *tomo* 'volume'
tls	typed letter signed
trans. (tr.)	translated by, translator, translation; transitive
ts., tss.	typescript, typescripts (cf. "ms.")
U	University; Fr. *Université, Universitaire*; Ger. *Universität*; Ital. *Università, Universitario, Universitaria*; Sp. *Universidad* (used in documentation; see "UP")
UP	University Press (used in documentation: Columbia UP)
usu.	usually
usw.	Ger. *und so weiter* 'and so on'
v	*verso* 'lefthand page'
[v.]	*vide* 'see'
v., vv. (vs., vss.)	verse, verses (cf. "vs. (v.)")
var.	variant
vb.	verb
[v.d.]	various dates
vgl.	Ger. *vergleiche* 'compare'
v.i.	verb intransitive
[viz.]	*videlicet* 'namely'
voc.	vocative

vol., vols.	volume, volumes
vs. (v.)	versus 'against' (v. preferred in titles of legal cases; cf. "v., vv.")
v.t.	verb transitive
writ.	written by, writer
z.B.	Ger. *zum Beispiel* 'for example'

6.5. Publishers' names

6.5.1. General guidelines

Shortened forms of publishers' names are included in the list of works cited, immediately after the city of publication, to enable the reader to locate a book or to acquire more information about it. Since publishers' addresses are listed in such books as *Books in Print*, *Literary Market Place*, and *International Literary Market Place*, you need give only enough information to enable your reader to look up the publisher in one of these sources. It is usually sufficient, for example, to give as the publisher's name "Harcourt" even if the title page indicates "Harcourt Brace Jovanovich" or one of the earlier names of that firm (Harcourt; Harcourt, Brace; Harcourt, Brace, and World). If you are preparing a bibliographical study, however, or if publication history is important to your work, give the publisher's name in full.

In shortening publishers' names, keep in mind the following:

1. Omit articles, business abbreviations (e.g., Co., Corp., Inc., Ltd.), and descriptive words (e.g., Books, House, Press, Publishers, Casa Editrice, Editions, Editura, Librairie, Libri, Verlag). When citing a university press, however, always add the abbreviation "P" (e.g., Ohio State UP) because the university itself may publish independently of its press (e.g., Ohio State U).

2. If the publisher's name includes the name of one person, cite the last name alone (e.g., Abrams, Heath, Norton, Wiley). If the publisher's name includes the names of more than one person, cite only the first of these names (e.g, Bobbs, Dodd, Faber, Farrar, Funk, Grosset, Harcourt, Harper, Holt, Houghton, McGraw, Prentice, Simon).

3. Use standard abbreviations whenever possible (e.g., Acad., Assn., Soc., UP).

4. If the publisher's name is commonly abbreviated with capital in-
    itial letters and if the abbreviation is likely to be familiar to your
    audience, use the abbreviation as the publisher's name (e.g., CAL,
    CNRS, EETS, MLA, NCTE, PUF, UMI). If your readers are
    not likely to know the abbreviation, shorten the name according
    to the general guidelines given above (e.g., Mod. Lang. Assn.).

6.5.2. Selected publishers' names

Acceptable shortened forms of publishers' names include the following:

Abrams	Harry N. Abrams, Inc.
Acad. for Educ. Dev.	Academy for Educational Development, Inc.
Aguilar	Aguilar Ediciones
Alianza	Alianza Editorial
Allen	George Allen and Unwin Publishers, Inc.
Allyn	Allyn and Bacon, Inc.
Almqvist	Almqvist och Wiksell Förlag
Appleton	Appleton-Century-Crofts
Athenäum	Athenäum Verlag
Barnes	Barnes and Noble Books
Basic	Basic Books
Beacon	Beacon Press, Inc.
Beck	Verlag C. H. Beck
Benn	Ernest Benn, Ltd.
Bertrand	Livraria Bertrand
Bobbs	The Bobbs-Merrill Co., Inc.
Botas	Libreria y Ediciones Botas
Bowker	R. R. Bowker Co.
Brasilia	Editora Brasilia
CAL	Center for Applied Linguistics
Cambridge UP	Cambridge University Press
Casalini	Casalini Libri
Clarendon	Clarendon Press
CNRS	Editions du Centre National de la Recherche Scientifique
Colin	Armand Colin, Editeur
Columbia UP	Columbia University Press
Cornell UP	Cornell University Press

Dell	Dell Publishing Co., Inc.
Didier	Librairie Marcel Didier
Dodd	Dodd, Mead, and Co.
Doubleday	Doubleday and Co., Inc.
Dover	Dover Publications, Inc.
Dutton	E. P. Dutton, Inc.
EETS	Early English Text Society
Farrar	Farrar, Straus, and Giroux, Inc.
Feminist	The Feminist Press
Free	The Free Press
Funk	Funk and Wagnalls, Inc.
Gale	Gale Research Co.
Garnier	Editions Garnier Frères
GPO	Government Printing Office
Gruyter	Walter de Gruyter and Co.
Harcourt	Harcourt Brace Jovanovich, Inc.
Harper	Harper and Row Publishers, Inc.
Harvard Law Rev. Assn.	Harvard Law Review Association
Harvard UP	Harvard University Press
Heath	D. C. Heath and Co.
HMSO	Her (His) Majesty's Stationery Office
Holt	Holt, Rinehart, and Winston, Inc.
Houghton	Houghton Mifflin Co.
Humanities	Humanities Press, Inc.
Indiana UP	Indiana University Press
Johns Hopkins UP	The Johns Hopkins University Press
Knopf	Alfred A. Knopf, Inc.
Larousse	Librairie Larousse
Laterza	Giuseppe Laterza e Figli
Le Monnier	Casa Editrice Felice Le Monnier
Lidové	Lidové nakladatelství
Lippincott	J. B. Lippincott Co.
Little	Little, Brown, and Co.
Lunde	Lunde Forlag og Bokhandel
Macmillan	Macmillan Publishing Co., Inc.
McGraw	McGraw-Hill, Inc.
MIT P	The MIT Press
MLA	The Modern Language Association of America
NAL	The New American Library, Inc.
Nauka	Izdatelstvo Nauka

NCTE	The National Council of Teachers of English
NEA	The National Education Association
New York Graphic Soc.	New York Graphic Society
Norton	W. W. Norton and Co., Inc.
Oveja	Editorial La Oveja Negra
Oxford UP	Oxford University Press, Inc.
Penguin	Penguin Books, Inc.
Popular	The Popular Press
Prentice	Prentice-Hall, Inc.
Princeton UP	Princeton University Press
PU de Lyon	Presses universitaires de Lyon
PU du Québec	Presses de l'Université du Québec
PUF	Presses universitaires de France
Putnam's	G. P. Putnam's Sons
Rand	Rand McNally and Co.
Random	Random House, Inc.
Rizzoli	Rizzoli Editore
St. Martin's	St. Martin's Press, Inc.
Scott	Scott, Foresman, and Co.
Scribner's	Charles Scribner's Sons
Simon	Simon and Schuster, Inc.
State U of New York P	State University of New York Press
UMI	University Microfilms International
U of Chicago P	University of Chicago Press
U of Toronto P	University of Toronto Press
UP of Florida	The University Presses of Florida
UTET	Unione Tipografico-Editrice Torinese
Viking	The Viking Press, Inc.
Yale UP	Yale University Press

6.6. Literary and religious works

The following are examples of abbreviations that may be used in documentation. It is usually best to introduce an abbreviation in parentheses immediately after the first use of the full title in the text: In *Paradise Lost* (*PL*), Milton. . . . For works not on these lists, follow prevailing practice or devise simple, unambiguous abbreviations of your own.

6.6.1. Bible (Bib.)

The following abbreviations and spelled forms are commonly used for parts of the Bible.

Old Testament (OT)

Gen.	Genesis
Exod.	Exodus
Lev.	Leviticus
Num.	Numbers
Deut.	Deuteronomy
Josh.	Joshua
Judg.	Judges
Ruth	Ruth
1 Sam.	1 Samuel
2 Sam.	2 Samuel
1 Kings	1 Kings
2 Kings	2 Kings
1 Chron.	1 Chronicles
2 Chron.	2 Chronicles
Ezra	Ezra
Neh.	Nehemiah
Esth.	Esther
Job	Job
Ps.	Psalms
Prov.	Proverbs
Eccles.	Ecclesiastes
Song Sol. (also Cant.)	Song of Solomon (also Canticles)
Isa.	Isaiah
Jer.	Jeremiah
Lam.	Lamentations
Ezek.	Ezekiel
Dan.	Daniel
Hos.	Hosea
Joel	Joel
Amos	Amos
Obad.	Obadiah
Jon.	Jonah
Mic.	Micah

Nah.	Nahum
Hab.	Habakkuk
Zeph.	Zephaniah
Hag.	Haggai
Zech.	Zechariah
Mal.	Malachi

Selected Apocryphal and Deuterocanonical Works

1 Esd.	1 Esdras
2 Esd.	2 Esdras
Tob.	Tobit
Jth.	Judith
Esth. (Apocr.)	Esther (Apocrypha)
Wisd. Sol. (also Wisd.)	Wisdom of Solomon (also Wisdom)
Ecclus. (also Sir.)	Ecclesiasticus (also Sirach)
Bar.	Baruch
Song 3 Childr.	Song of the Three Children
Sus.	Susanna
Bel and Dr.	Bel and the Dragon
Pr. Man.	Prayer of Manasseh
1 Macc.	1 Maccabees
2 Macc.	2 Maccabees

New Testament (NT)

Matt.	Matthew
Mark	Mark
Luke	Luke
John	John
Acts	Acts
Rom.	Romans
1 Cor.	1 Corinthians
2 Cor.	2 Corinthians
Gal.	Galatians
Eph.	Ephesians

Phil.	Philippians
Col.	Colossians
1 Thess.	1 Thessalonians
2 Thess.	2 Thessalonians
1 Tim.	1 Timothy
2 Tim.	2 Timothy
Tit.	Titus
Philem.	Philemon
Heb.	Hebrews
Jas.	James
1 Pet.	1 Peter
2 Pet.	2 Peter
1 John	1 John
2 John	2 John
3 John	3 John
Jude	Jude
Rev. (also Apoc.)	Revelation (also Apocalypse)

Selected Apocryphal Works

G. Thom.	Gospel of Thomas
G. Heb.	Gospel of the Hebrews
G. Pet.	Gospel of Peter

6.6.2.   Shakespeare

Ado	*Much Ado about Nothing*
Ant.	*Antony and Cleopatra*
AWW	*All's Well That Ends Well*
AYL	*As You Like It*
Cor.	*Coriolanus*
Cym.	*Cymbeline*
Err.	*The Comedy of Errors*
F1	First Folio ed. (1623)
F2	Second Folio ed. (1632)
Ham.	*Hamlet*
1H4	*Henry IV, Part 1*
2H4	*Henry IV, Part 2*
H5	*Henry V*

1H6	*Henry VI, Part 1*
2H6	*Henry VI, Part 2*
3H6	*Henry VI, Part 3*
H8	*Henry VIII*
JC	*Julius Caesar*
Jn.	*King John*
LC	*A Lover's Complaint*
LLL	*Love's Labour's Lost*
Lr.	*King Lear*
Luc.	*The Rape of Lucrece*
Mac.	*Macbeth*
MM	*Measure for Measure*
MND	*A Midsummer Night's Dream*
MV	*The Merchant of Venice*
Oth.	*Othello*
Per.	*Pericles*
PhT	*The Phoenix and the Turtle*
PP	*The Passionate Pilgrim*
Q	Quarto ed.
R2	*Richard II*
R3	*Richard III*
Rom.	*Romeo and Juliet*
Shr.	*The Taming of the Shrew*
Son.	*Sonnets*
TGV	*The Two Gentlemen of Verona*
Tim.	*Timon of Athens*
Tit.	*Titus Andronicus*
Tmp.	*The Tempest*
TN	*Twelfth Night*
TNK	*The Two Noble Kinsmen*
Tro.	*Troilus and Cressida*
Ven.	*Venus and Adonis*
Wiv.	*The Merry Wives of Windsor*
WT	*The Winter's Tale*

6.6.3. Chaucer

CkT	The Cook's Tale
ClT	The Clerk's Tale
CT	*The Canterbury Tales*
CYT	The Canon's Yeoman's Tale

FranT	The Franklin's Tale
FrT	The Friar's Tale
GP	The General Prologue
KnT	The Knight's Tale
ManT	The Manciple's Tale
Mel	The Tale of Melibee
MerT	The Merchant's Tale
MilT	The Miller's Tale
MkT	The Monk's Tale
MLT	The Man of Law's Tale
NPT	The Nun's Priest's Tale
PardT	The Pardoner's Tale
ParsT	The Parson's Tale
PhyT	The Physician's Tale
PrT	The Prioress's Tale
Ret	Chaucer's Retraction
RvT	The Reeve's Tale
ShT	The Shipman's Tale
SNT	The Second Nun's Tale
SqT	The Squire's Tale
SumT	The Summoner's Tale
Th	The Tale of Sir Thopas
WBT	The Wife of Bath's Tale

6.7. Languages

Abbreviations for languages are used not only in documentation but also in the text of linguistic studies where the context makes them clear. Periods are not used in abbreviations containing all capital letters (ME), but a period follows an abbreviation ending in a lowercase letter (Chin.). For a linguistic abbreviation that joins one or more abbreviations ending in lowercase letters, only one period appears, by convention, at the end of the combined abbreviation; no space is left between the two terms (OFr., AmerInd.).

AFr.	Anglo-French
Afrik.	Afrikaans
Alb.	Albanian
AmerInd.	American Indian

AmerSp.	American Spanish
AN	Anglo-Norman
Ar.	Arabic
Arab.	Arabian
Aram.	Aramaic
Arm.	Armenian
Assyr.	Assyrian
Bab.	Babylonian
Beng.	Bengali
Bret.	Breton
Bulg.	Bulgarian
CanFr.	Canadian French
Cant.	Cantonese
Catal.	Catalan
Celt.	Celtic
Chin.	Chinese
Dan.	Danish
Du.	Dutch
E, Eng.	English
Egypt.	Egyptian
Esk.	Eskimo
Finn.	Finnish
Flem.	Flemish
Fr.	French
Fris.	Frisian
G, Ger.	German
Gael.	Gaelic
Gk.	Greek
Goth.	Gothic
Heb.	Hebrew
HG	High German
Hung.	Hungarian
Icel.	Icelandic
IE	Indo-European
Ind.	Indian
Ir.	Irish
It.	Italian
Jap.	Japanese
L	Late (e.g., LGk., LHeb., LL); Low (e.g., LG)
L, Lat.	Latin
LaFr.	Louisiana French

M	Medieval (e.g., ML); Middle (e.g., ME, MFlem., MHG, MLG)
MexSp.	Mexican Spanish
N	New (e.g., NGk., NHeb., NL); Norse
Norw.	Norwegian
O	Old (e.g., OE, OFr., OHG, ON, OProv., OS)
PaGer.	Pennsylvania German
Pek.	Pekingese
Per.	Persian
PhilSp.	Philippine Spanish
Pol.	Polish
Port.	Portuguese
Prov.	Provençal
Pruss.	Prussian
Rom.	Romanian
Russ.	Russian
S	Saxon
Scand.	Scandinavian
Scot.	Scottish
Skt.	Sanskrit
Slav.	Slavic
Sp.	Spanish
Swed.	Swedish
Syr.	Syriac
Tag.	Tagalog
Turk.	Turkish
VL	Vulgar Latin
W	Welsh

6.8.   Proofreading symbols

Proofreading symbols with marginal corrections are used when correcting galley proof and page proof; corrections should never be given in the margins of a manuscript. (On correcting proof, see 1.7.4.) A list of proofreading symbols and a sample of their application follow. The symbols are divided into two sections: those used in the text and those used in the margin. Every symbol used in the text requires a corresponding symbol or notation in the margin.

6.8.1.   Symbols used in the text

/   (1) error (err/r), with correction in the margin

(2) lowercase (d∅g), with "lc" within a circle in the margin

⌒   close up (is⌒land); repeat symbol in the margin

𝒯   delete and close up a single letter (c𝒯at), with delete and close up symbol in the margin

├──┤   delete and close up more than one letter (the important ~~important~~/point); with delete and close up symbol in the margin

∧   insert (in∧ert), with the insertion in the margin

∨   set as superscript (3∨); repeat symbol in the margin

ↄ∩   transpose elements (th∩e, in⌐beginning⌐the), with "tr" within a circle in the margin

⬭   (1) material to be corrected, with the correction in the margin

(2) material to be moved, with its new location specified in the margin

(3) spell out, with spelled form or "sp" within a circle in the margin

══   straighten (placed over and under words); repeat symbol in the margin

6.8.2.   Symbols used in the margin

/   (1) separates more than one correction in a line (♫/#)

(2) indicates correction to be made more than once (♫//)

∅   (3) indicates numeral 0, not letter O

⌒   close up

𝒹   delete

ℛ	delete and close up
ⓣⓡ	transpose
#	space
(more #)	more space
(less #)	less space
⊙	period
⌃	comma
⊖	colon
⌃;	semicolon
⌄	(1) apostrophe
	(2) single closing quotation mark
⌄	single opening quotation mark
⌄ ⌄	double quotation marks
( )	parentheses
[ ]	square brackets
/	slash
=	hyphen
⅟M	one-em dash
2⁄M	two-em dash
⅟N	one-en dash
≡	capital letter (placed under letter)
(cap)	capital letter
=	small capital letter (placed under letter)
(sc)	small capital letter
(lc)	lowercase
(ital)	italics
(rom)	roman
(bf)	boldface
(sp)	spell out
¶	paragraph
(no ¶)	no paragraph

⌐—— move to left

——⌐ move to right

⌐ ⌐ move up

⌐ ⌐ move down

= straighten lines

// align vertically

(stet) let stand as is

(wf) wrong font

(X) broken letter or dirty proof

6.8.3.   Sample marked proof

"Now, what I want is Facts. Teach these boys and girls nothing (tr)/⌐/#
but Facts. Facts alone are are wanted in life. Plant nothing (lc)/ʒ/ʒ
else and root out everything else. You can only form the u/o
(tr)/⌐ minds reasoning of animals upon facts nothing else will ever (cap)/θ
be of any sevice to them. This is the principle on which I bring r/#
ʒ/⌐ up my own up my own children, and this is the principle on
which I bring up these children. Stick to the Facts, sir! ⌐/ʒ/ⱱ

7 PREPARATION OF THESES AND DISSERTATIONS

7.1. General

Before beginning work on a thesis or dissertation, inquire about the specific requirements of your department, school, or university. The following sections describe common, though not universal, practices in preparing such manuscripts. Consult the appropriate sections of earlier chapters for information applicable to all scholarly writing.

7.2. Selection of a thesis topic

Because a thesis or dissertation often takes months or years to complete, choose a topic that you can work with for a considerable time. Innovative in either subject matter or method, the project should make a substantial contribution to your field. Preliminary discussions with instructors, especially the thesis adviser, should prove invaluable to you in making your selection. Before presenting the topic for formal approval, verify its originality by identifying previous studies in the area. Consult all relevant sources for this information — the card catalog, bibliographies in the field, *DA* and *DAI*, the *Comprehensive Dissertation Index*, and listings of foreign dissertations. This step helps not only to modify and redefine the topic but also to provide the basic bibliography for the thesis. Your thesis adviser and other professors can assist you in defining objectives, setting the limits of research, testing the soundness of arguments and conclusions, and improving the bibliography.

7.3. Thesis prospectus or outline

An important stage between the selection and approval of the thesis topic and the writing of the thesis is the preparation of a detailed prospectus or outline. Often this document, usually accompanied by a preliminary bibliography, must receive the approval of the thesis adviser, the thesis committee, the entire department, and the dean of the graduate school as well.

7.4. Pagination

Use lowercase roman numerals in paginating the preliminary parts of the thesis or dissertation — including title page, copyright page, dedication (optional), epigraph (optional), table of contents, lists of illustrations and tables (if applicable), preface, and acknowledgments (often combined with the preface). Use arabic numerals in paginating the text and the bibliography as well as any endnotes and, if applicable, the appendix, glossary, and index. (See 3.3.1 for the order of the divisions of the text.) Although all pages, beginning with the title page, count in the total enumeration of the work, the title page and the copyright page usually do not bear numbers. Page numbers should appear on all other pages. If you present an abstract of the thesis or dissertation, place it before the title page but do not include it in the pagination.

7.5. Special requirements for theses and dissertations

In modern scholarship, theses and dissertations, which are generally recorded on microfilm, qualify as forms of publication in themselves. Their pages therefore should resemble those of a printed book as closely as possible.

Because dissertations are most often read in their microfilm versions, it is essential to include enough documentation in the text to keep the reader from constantly having to roll the film to the list of works cited. See 5.2-3 for techniques of incorporating information in the text.

Unlike a research paper, the thesis or dissertation must have a formal title page. The title page usually includes the title, the author, the thesis adviser, a statement indicating that the work has been submitted in partial fulfillment of degree requirements, and the date. Do not underline the title, put it in quotation marks, or capitalize it in full (see 2.2.8 for the appropriate use of underlining). Consult your department or graduate office about the exact format of the page, since requirements vary from school to school.

Double-space the text of the dissertation. Unless otherwise instructed, however, single-space all passages of verse and prose set off from the text, all entries in the list of works cited, and any notes. Skip a line between bibliographic citations and between notes (to allow for raising the note number a half line). Since most dissertations are now microfilmed, whatever notes are necessary usually appear individually at the bottoms of the relevant pages rather than grouped together at the end of the work.

Dissertations should be free of typing errors and bound in accordance with departmental or graduate school regulations. Leave one-inch margins at the top, bottom, and right side of each page, but indent the text two inches from the left to allow for binding. Type chapter titles one inch from the top of the page.

Some departments and schools require the use of special thesis paper with preprinted margins. The department or graduate office also usually furnishes information on the registration of copyright for the dissertation, the publication of an abstract of the dissertation in *DAI* (600 words or fewer), and the microfilming of the work by University Microfilms International (300 North Zeeb Road, Ann Arbor, MI 48106).

7.6. Permissions

Since theses and dissertations are considered published works, consult the section on permissions (1.9.2).

INDEX

References are to section numbers. Definitions of abbreviations are found in chapter 6; section numbers given for individual abbreviations locate discussions of their uses.

assignment of rights in contracts,
   1.7.1(1)
Association of American Publishers,
   3.5.3, 3.5.5
audience, 1.1
author-date system of parenthetical
   documentation, 5.7.1
author-publisher relations, guidelines
   for, 1.8
authors
  corporate
    in bibliographies, 4.5.6
    in notes, 5.8.5d
    in parenthetical documentation,
     5.5.5
  multiple
    in bibliographies
     multiple works by, 4.5.5
     one work by, 4.5.4
    in notes, 5.8.5c
    multiple works by, in parenthetical
     documentation, 5.5.6
  names of, 2.3.3
    in bibliographies, 4.4.2
    omitted, 4.7.8
    repeated, 4.5.3
    of government publications, in
     bibliographies, 4.5.17
    in notes, 5.8.3
    in parenthetical documentation,
     5.3, 5.4
    of periodical articles, in bibliog-
     raphies, 4.6.2
    of reference works, in bibliogra-
     phies, 4.5.15
    in subsequent note references,
     5.8.8
    transliterated, 2.3.13
  single
    in bibliographies
     multiple works by, 4.5.3
     one work by, 4.5.1
    in notes, 5.8.5a
authors' alterations
  costs of, in contracts, 1.7.1(6)
  to proofs, 1.7.4

authors' copies, agreements concerning, in contracts, 1.7.1(13)
authors' discounts, agreements concerning, in contracts,
   1.7.1(13)
authorship, doubtful, 4.4.2
Author's Primer to Word Processing, An,
   3.5.3, 3.5.5

ballets
  in bibliographies, 4.8.7
  in notes, 5.8.7g
  titles of, italics with, 2.5.2
Barzun, Jacques, 1.3
BC, in dates, 2.7.5
BCE, in dates, 2.7.5
Beardsley, Monroe C., 1.3
Belorussian, transliteration of, 2.8
Bengali, transliteration of, 2.8
Bernstein, Theodore, 1.3
Bible
  abbreviations of, 6.6.1
  citing chapter and verse, 5.5.8
  titles of books of, 2.5.5
  titles of versions of, 2.5.5
bibliographic citations
  periods with, 2.2.10
  question marks with, 2.2.11
bibliographic description, definition
   of, 4.1
bibliographic forms, in documentation, 5.8.3
bibliographic notes, with parenthetical documentation, 5.6.2
bibliographies *See also* works cited
  abbreviations in, 6, 6.4
  addresses (speeches) in, 4.8.14
  afterwords in, 4.5.9
  alphabetization of, 4.3
  annotated
    arrangement of, 4.3
    definition of, 4.1
  anthologies in, 4.5.2, 4.5.8
  archival recordings in, 4.8.5
  arrangement of, 4.3